New York City, 1664–1710

CONQUEST AND CHANGE

New York City, 1664–1710

CONQUEST AND CHANGE

Thomas J. Archdeacon

Cornell University Press

ITHACA AND LONDON

Cornell University Press gratefully acknowledges
a grant from the Andrew J. Mellon Foundation
that aided in bringing this book to publication.

First published 1976 by Cornell University Press.
Published in the United Kingdom by Cornell University Press Ltd.,
2-4 Brook Street, London W1Y 1AA.

International Standard Book Number 0-8014-0944-6
Library of Congress Catalog Card Number 75-22893
Printed in the United States of America by Vail-Ballou Press, Inc.

*To my mother and the
memory of my father*

❦ Preface

Writing about the colonial period of United States history presents historians with a special problem. Unlike scholars concerned with the Revolution or later eras, they must deal with at least thirteen separate entities rather than a single nation. Narratives about individual provinces provide indispensable information for the specialist, but of necessity they offer a fragmented image of the colonial past. To readers more familiar with the national scope of histories of later times, such studies must seem quite parochial.

In order to develop themes with general content, many historians have attempted instead to uncover social processes and developmental patterns common to the colonial experience. Taking advantage of the small populations in provincial settlements, some scholars have culled the vital records of single communities to construct detailed accounts of colonial life. Through study of two elemental units of society, the family and the village, they have hoped to find the essence of early America. Their investigations, which often have had a demographic orientation, rank with the most creative research of recent years, but the approach they have chosen has disadvantages.

Though examinations of individual towns have led to the formulation of provocative theses, this approach logically requires the completion of many such studies before generalizations can be safely made about colonial society. Unfortunately, circumstances are not propitious for the conduct of a sufficient number of these investigations. The research can be tedious and repetitive; scholars who have completed projects of this type have subsequently turned to fresh areas of endeavor. And imaginative graduate students, especially in a period of economic crisis, are reluctant to limit themselves to replicating earlier works.

Moreover, this type of research is best suited to the study of settlements of modest size for which ample sources are available. This tendency has been beneficial insofar as it has brought needed attention to towns and villages of the type in which the great majority of colonists lived. But it has also produced a hesitance on the part of scholars to study larger communities, which had a disproportionately greater impact on society but whose records are often complex and incomplete.

In this book I have tried to apply techniques associated with community studies to research on a major colonial city, New York. The advantages of studying a community whose history is of prime importance outweigh the dangers of depending on sources of uneven quality. In particular, this approach affords a new means of investigating political and social phenomena of broad significance.

Primarily, this book is an examination of the aftermath of the English capture of New York City from the Dutch. Historians have treated the take-over as a simple change of international jurisdiction, the consequences of which were of little import to the community. I believe, however, that the conquest produced basic social, economic, and political changes, which in turn laid the foundation for the tumultuous events of the closing years of the seventeenth century.

In broader terms, the book is an analysis of the factors underlying the political behavior of ordinary colonists. I have searched for the issues which, in an age of political deference to the wealthy and well-born, could produce controversy and popular excitement. My conclusions indicate that early New Yorkers responded to stimuli surprisingly similar to those affecting American citizens in the nineteenth and twentieth centuries.

The results of my investigations, I believe, justify the study of colonial urban society from a community perspective. And they suggest that historians should shift their focus from New England to the middle colonies and particularly to the cities of New York and Philadelphia. Indeed, the experiences of these provinces may hold the key to the origin of the democratic ethos and institutions of America.

Many people gave me valuable guidance as I worked on this book. They fit into the overlapping categories of teachers, friends, and family. All of them deserve credit for whatever strong points the study may have; none deserve blame for its weaknesses.

My admiration for and gratitude to Richard B. Morris of Columbia University are profound. Incisive, witty, and kind, he knows how to apportion direction and freedom, criticism and encouragement. The diversity of interests among Professor Morris's students is obvious testimony to his breadth of knowledge.

Michael Kammen of Cornell University, from his first reading of the manuscript which evolved into this book, has given unstintingly of advice and assistance. Professor Kammen's efforts have been an example of the finest traditions of scholarly cooperation.

Stuart Bruchey, Kenneth Jackson, James S. Young, and the late Wallace Sayre of Columbia University, and Pauline Maier of the University of Massachusetts at Boston made prudent and constructive suggestions. Patricia Bonomi of New York University, Lawrence Leder of Lehigh University, and Jackson Turner Main of the State University of New York at Stony Brook offered useful comments when I presented papers dealing with phases of the research. John Murrin of Princeton University has been generous with advice and encouragement.

Colonels Thomas Griess, Amos Jordan, Roger Nye, and Lee Don Olvey supported my efforts to complete my research while I served in the Army as a member of the faculty at the United States Military Academy at West Point. The Department of History at the University of Wisconsin has provided a congenial and stimulating environment. I especially appreciate the interest Allan Bogue, Paul Conkin, Merrill Jensen, and David Lovejoy have shown in my endeavors.

The staffs of many institutions have made the work easier and more efficient. I want in particular to thank the persons who eased my labors at the Hall of Records, the Criminal Court Library, the Historic Documents Collection at Klapper Library, Queens College, City University of New York, the Special Collections of Butler Library at Columbia University, the New-York Historical Society, the New York Public Library, the New York Genealogical and Biographical Society, and the Wisconsin Historical Society.

I would like to thank the Board of Regents of the State of New York for awarding me College Teaching and Herbert Lehman Fellowships, and I would like to express my appreciation to the Woodrow Wilson Foundation for a dissertation fellowship. Without these awards, completion of the research would have been much more difficult.

My wife, Marilyn Lavin, has given unselfishly of her time and talent. She has pursued her own doctorate in history, been a fine mother to our children, and helped me in every way possible. Her criticisms were at times the hardest to accept because her approval meant the most to me. I only hope that I have done justice to her acute suggestions, and that I can be of as much assistance to her in her work.

Our children are too small to understand research and writing. But they also helped. Meghan, Patrick, and Caitlin put the work in perspective and made me aware of the more important things in life.

T. J. A.

Madison, Wisconsin

ॐ *Contents*

↝ Maps

↝ Figures

Tables

❦ *Abbreviations*

Col. Laws   *The Colonial Laws of New York, from the Year 1664 to the Revolution.* Vol. I.

Coll. HSA   *Collections of the Huguenot Society of America.* Vol. I: *Registers of the Births, Marriages, and Deaths in the "Eglise Françoise à la Nouvelle York," from 1683 to 1804.* Edited by [Rev.] Alfred V. Wittmeyer.

Coll. NYGBS   *Collections of the New York Genealogical and Biographical Society.* Vol. II: *Baptisms from 1639 to 1730 in the Dutch Reformed Church: New Amsterdam and New York City.* Vol. IX: *Marriages from 1639 to 1801 in the Reformed Dutch Church: New Amsterdam and New York City.*

Coll. NYHS   *Collections of the New-York Historical Society.*

Con. Lib.   Conveyance Libers, Hall of Records, New York.

DHNY   *Documentary History of the State of New York.* Edited by Edmund B. O'Callaghan.

DRNY   *Documents Relative to the Colonial History of the State of New York.* Edited by Edmund B. O'Callaghan.

HMR   *An Account of Her Majesty's Revenue in the Province of New York, 1701–1709: The Customs Records of Early Colonial New York.* Edited by Julius M. Bloch *et al.*

Min. Com. Coun.   *Minutes of the Common Council of the City of New York, 1675–1776.* Edited by Herbert Levi Osgood.

Min. Ves.   Minutes of the Vestry. Trinity Church, New York. Vol. I (1697–1791).

NYGB Rec.   *New York Genealogical and Biographical Record.*

WMQ   *William and Mary Quarterly,* third series.

New York City, 1664–1710

CONQUEST AND CHANGE

1 ✑ The Importance of the Middle Colonies

By applying analytic techniques adopted from the social sciences to new topics of investigation, students of the colonial period have made their field an exciting area of historical research. Inspired by English demographers,[1] a group of American scholars has developed a modern version of the "new social history." Some have focused on the family and on rural communal life in early America. Others have begun to chart with long needed precision the distribution of wealth in the provinces and the prospects of upward mobility.

Large dividends have already been derived from these efforts, but they are not immune from problems. The historians of seventeenth and eighteenth century American communities have produced a "model" of provincial society which differs in critical respects from that conceived by those studying economic stratification. As a result, these two groups have proposed or implied explanations of popular responses to political events that are at least partially incompatible with each other and with findings about the basis of such behavior in later eras.

[1] For example, Peter Laslett, *The World We Have Lost* (New York, 1965); Peter Laslett and John Harrison, "Clayworth and Cogenhoe," in H. E. Bell and R. L. Ollard, eds., *Historical Essays, 1600–1750: Presented to David Ogg* (London, 1963), pp. 157–184; D. V. Glass and D. E. C. Eversley, eds., *Population in History: Essays in Historical Demography* (Chicago, 1965); E. A. Wrigley, ed., *An Introduction to English Historical Demography from the Sixteenth to the Nineteenth Century* (London, 1966).

Works by political historians have not been able to reconcile the discordant theses put forward by the "new social historians." Colonial scholars among the quantitatively-oriented "new political historians" have concentrated their attention on leadership elites and on legislative institutions. They have not taken the same approach as the social historians, whose examinations try to encompass all elements of the population, or as those traditional political historians who have sought through nonquantitative means to uncover the role of the inarticulate. Not having systematically scrutinized the behavior of ordinary men and women, they do not provide a theory to unite the divergent models of the new social history.

Kenneth Lockridge and Philip Greven have produced fine examples of the new social history in their books about the colonial communities of Dedham and Andover, Massachusetts, respectively.[2] Though different in methods and goals, and appreciative of the peculiarities of each town's history, their analyses of social and economic life are strikingly similar. Established in 1636, Dedham enjoyed great success for half a century. But the stable original settlers eventually died, and even worse, land reserves were exhausted by 1713. Time also overtook Andover, which was founded in 1646 and likewise experienced early prosperity followed by an era of shortages. By the middle of the eighteenth century both Dedham and Andover were faced with unprecedented amounts of out-migration as the continued natural growth in population reduced individual land holdings below an acceptable level.

"Generation" is the most important analytic concept to have

[2] Kenneth Lockridge, *A New England Town, The First Hundred Years: Dedham, Massachusetts, 1636–1736* (New York, 1970); Philip J. Greven, Jr., *Four Generations: Population, Land, and Family in Colonial Andover, Massachusetts* (Ithaca, N.Y., 1970).

emerged from the research of Lockridge and Greven.[3] They are not alone in categorizing their subjects by generation rather than by some other characteristic. John Demos's work on Plymouth Colony emphasized intergenerational relations, and he has argued that family tensions, especially between mothers and daughters, helped create the witch hysteria in Salem, Massachusetts. After assaying the writings of Lockridge, Greven, and Demos, John Murrin has suggested that opposition to the Halfway Covenant was a tactic of the Puritan founders, who used the fates of their grandchildren's souls as a potent psychological weapon to stimulate the second generation to duplicate their conversion experiences.[4]

A generational analysis of society seriously affects the interpretation of politics. Unless constant antagonism between parents and children is the order of the world, it must assume that schisms within the population will be infrequent. The divisions that do occur will follow lines of age rather than of the social and economic cleavages usually prominent in historical analysis, and differences will always be resolvable since the older generation will eventually die. More often, however, a

[3] Demographers might object to the use of the word "generation," which technically refers to persons born in the same "cohorts" or intervals of years. They can argue that the citizens of Dedham and Andover were residents of towns which were passing through several "stages of development," and indeed Lockridge himself has written in favor of this concept ("Land, Population and the Evolution of New England Society, 1630–1790," *Past and Present,* no. 39 [Apr. 1968] pp. 62–80). For the purposes of this analysis either term, generation or stage of development, is acceptable because both assume that the whole population, or large segments of it distinguishable by age, share the most important historical experiences as a unit.

[4] John Demos, *A Little Commonwealth: Family Life in Plymouth Colony* (New York, 1970); John Demos, "Underlying Themes in the Witchcraft of Seventeenth Century New England," *American Historical Review,* LXXX (June 1970), 1311–26; John Murrin, "Review Essay," *History and Theory,* XI (1972), 226–75.

unified people will relieve the inevitable tensions associated with social and economic change by a purging ritual or by a hostile outburst against an outside agent believed to be responsible for the difficulties.

Although not labeled as such, the generational or "communal" interpretation of politics has become common in treatments of early America. The approach is persuasive because it offers a rationale for the widely accepted notion that the colonial era lacked political parties. On-going partisan organizations thrive on permanent or long-lasting divisions within the populace, but from the generational perspective time resolves all differences. The inevitable victory of the younger generation seems to be the corollary of Murrin's comments on the Halfway Covenant. In less extreme situations physical expansion of the community or migration of the young will ease tensions. Lockridge's and Sumner C. Powell's analyses of the growth of new villages around Dedham and Sudbury, Massachusetts, attest to the existence of this process.[5]

The generational interpretation can also explain major events like the Great Awakening. Richard Bushman's optimistic description of the prosperity of some eighteenth century communities differs from the darker portrayals by Lockridge and Greven, but his Connecticut Yankees apparently underwent inner struggles analogous to those experienced in Massachusetts. Puritans pursuing mammon, they were caught between prevailing economic realities and older religious ideals, until the Awakening, a cathartic episode of humiliation and rebirth, enabled them to erase the unbearable guilt.[6]

Even the American Revolution can fit into the generational

[5] Lockridge, *New England Town,* ch. 6; Sumner C. Powell, *Puritan Village: The Formation of a New England Town* (Middletown, Conn., 1963).

[6] Richard L. Bushman, *From Puritan to Yankee: Character and the Social Order in Connecticut, 1690–1775* (Cambridge, Mass., 1967).

schema. Lockridge notes that the colonists never lost the utopian urge which gave Dedham its spirit. In such a framework the Revolution can be interpreted as a cleansing and revivifying experience by which a unified people reacted to the fear that their society was beginning to resemble that of Europe. Michael Zuckerman, whose controversial work describes the unity of a colonial society, likewise sees the Revolution as a response to English threats upon a cherished communal way of life.[7]

At first impression, the studies of economic stratification in colonial America lend support to the theories of the generational or communal school. Both agree that the eighteenth century was a time of increasing economic inequality. James Henretta, James Lemon and Gary Nash, and Aubrey Land, in their respective examinations of Boston, Pennsylvania's Chester County, and the northern Chesapeake, demonstrate that, as the provincial era passed, the rich in each area accumulated a larger share of the available assets. The people of middle and low rank became at least relatively less prosperous, and the percentage of propertyless citizens increased.[8]

Closer comparison shows that the investigators of economic stratification diverge from the community historians in fundamental respects. Working in the tradition of the Progressives they reject descriptions which stress the pervasiveness of consensus in early America. In so far as the "neo-Progressives"

[7] Lockridge, *New England Town,* ch. 9; Michael Zuckerman, *Peaceable Kingdoms: New England Towns in the Eighteenth Century* (New York, 1970), ch. 7.

[8] James A. Henretta, "Economic Development and Social Structure in Colonial Boston," *WMQ,* XXII (Jan. 1965), 75–92; James T. Lemon and Gary B. Nash, "The Distribution of Wealth in Eighteenth-Century America: A Century of Change in Chester County, Pennsylvania, 1693–1802," *Journal of Social History,* II (Jan. 1968), 1–24; Aubrey C. Land, "Economic Base and Social Structure: The Northern Chesapeake in the Eighteenth Century," *Journal of Economic History,* XXV (Dec. 1965), 639–54.

relate their conclusions to politics, they proceed from the assumption that inequities in the distribution of wealth cause serious conflict in society, and that perceptions of class rather than of generation underlie popular political attitudes.

Recent examinations of colonial politics do not resolve the discrepancies between the generational and economic approaches. Historians using traditional methods make the assumption that the ordinary citizen either shared the same aspiration as the provincial leadership or that they independently pursued class interests.[9] The few "new political historians" studying pre-Revolutionary America have been primarily interested in the formation and functions of elites. Their analyses of voting in the assemblies indicate that the issues tended to be sectional, but this finding has little direct significance for discerning grass root divisions in an era when all elections were local.[10] Presumably candidates from the same region would share the economic outlook of that area.

Unfortunately, the overall impact of the new social history has been to isolate interpretations of the colonial era from those of later periods. Doubtless the studies have discovered many of the unique qualities of provincial America, and further research into the typology of communities may show that generational

[9] For example, Robert M. Weir, " 'The Harmony We Were Famous For': An Interpretation of Pre-Revolutionary South Carolina Politics," *WMQ,* XXVI (Oct. 1969), 473–501; Bernard Bailyn, *The Ideological Origins of the American Revolution* (Cambridge, Mass., 1965); Jesse Lemisch, "Jack Tar in the Streets: Merchant Seamen in the Politics of Revolutionary America," *WMQ,* XXV (July 1968), 371–407; Jesse Lemisch, "The American Revolution Seen from the Bottom Up," in Barton Bernstein, ed., *Towards a New Past* (New York, 1968), pp. 3–45.

[10] For example, Robert M. Zemsky, "Power, Influence, and Status: Leadership Patterns in the Massachusetts Assembly, 1740–1755," *WMQ,* XXVI (Oct. 1969), 502–20; Jackson T. Main, *Political Parties before the Constitution* (Chapel Hill, N.C., 1973), ch. 1.

and economic approaches have their own appropriate applica-
tions. Nevertheless the image of provincial life presented in
these analyses obscures the roots of later American experience,
and does not explain why the continuation under the Republic of
social and economic divisions similar to those of the colonial
period produced such radically different political forms.

Independence did not dissipate the sources of tension discovered by the social historians of the colonies. Gordon Wood has
shown that the spirit of communal regeneration sought by the
revolutionaries did not last past the initial phase of the war.
Allan Kulikoff's study of Boston demonstrates that wealth became even more unevenly distributed after 1776, and Lemon
and Nash's extension of their Chester County data until 1802
shows a similar trend.[11]

Despite continuing societal problems, the type of politics
characteristic of post-Revolutionary America was remarkably
unlike that portrayed by colonial historians. In fact, partisan
politics flourished.[12] The alignments not only reflected sectional
disputes, but parties also found catalysts in local divisions, in
direct contrast to the colonial unity indicated by the generational
historians.

Data from the nineteenth century likewise make less persuasive the explanation of popular politics which underlies the
stratification studies. Using statistical tests to identify the deter-

[11] Gordon S. Wood, *The Creation of the American Republic, 1776–1787*
(Chapel Hill, 1969), pt. 4; Allan Kulikoff, "The Progress of Inequality in
Revolutionary Boston," *WMQ*, XXVIII (July 1971), 375–412; Lemon and
Nash, "Distribution of Wealth," pp. 1–24.

[12] See, for example, Noble Cunningham, *The Jeffersonian Republicans*
(Chapel Hill, N.C., 1957–63); David H. Fischer, *The Revolution of American
Conservatism: The Federalist Party in the Era of Jeffersonian Democracy*
(New York, 1965); James M. Banner, Jr., *To the Hartford Convention: The
Federalists and the Origins of Party Politics in Massachusetts, 1789–1815*
(New York, 1969).

minants of the electorate's behavior, "new political historians" like Richard McCormick have denied that class considerations were of primary importance. Scholars like Lee Benson, Robert Swierenga, and Richard Jensen have instead pointed to the importance of ethnocultural allegiances.[13]

Reconciling interpretations of the colonial era with interpretations of later eras is possible if scholars shift their focus of investigation and expand the number of factors which they take into consideration. The generational historians have concentrated their attention almost exclusively on Massachusetts, but during the early years of the Republic, New England revealed itself to have social ideals quite unlike those of other sections. On the other hand, the historians of class have analyzed only the role of economics and have neglected other potential influences on popular behavior.

The basis of social and political division in the middle colonies remained constant across the entire span of the American past. History is the study of what was beginning as well as of what was ending, and the middle colonies' early years were particularly relevant to the study of the development of later America. New York and Pennsylvania, the largest provinces in the region, were the spawning grounds of the first political parties in the United States, and almost from the beginning had heterogeneous populations more characteristic of nineteenth and twentieth century America. Indeed, as an English visitor com-

[13] Richard P. McCormick, "Suffrage Classes and Party Alignments: A Study in Voter Behavior," *Mississippi Valley Historical Review,* XLVI (Dec. 1959), 397–410; Lee Benson, *The Concept of Jacksonian Democracy: New York as a Test Case* (Princeton, N.J., 1961); Robert M. Swierenga, "Ethnocultural Political Analysis: A New Approach to American Ethnic Studies," *Journal of American Studies,* V (Apr. 1971), 59–79; Richard Jensen, "The Religious and Occupational Roots of Party Identification: Illinois and Indiana in the 1870s," *Civil War History,* XVI (Dec. 1970), 325–43.

mented in 1800, the middle colonies were ''never out of step in the national march.'' [14]

Even in its provincial phase, New York City exhibited the pluralism so typical of a later America, and this attribute has created conditions discouraging to scholars. New York lacks the consistency of politics, the sense of heritage, and the abundance of preserved records found in stable, homogeneous societies. Its labyrinthine politics and haphazard management of vital sources are ultimately the consequence of a tempestuous process of conflict and assimilation present from the beginning.

Neglect of New York history, though, obscures important elements of the American heritage. Ironically, the qualities which make the city difficult to study are the very ones which make the examination mandatory. Historians must recognize that sources, albeit imperfect, do exist. They must value the subject more than the data, willingly recognize that descriptions of a city churning with vitality can never be as exact as those of comparatively stable villages, and confront again New York's colonial past.

This book attempts to make a harmonious combination of the ''new social'' and the ''new political'' histories.[15] It draws inspiration from its predecessors, borrows some techniques from them, and, I hope, makes a few worthwhile innovations. Although not an exercise in demography, the work approaches the history of New York City by means of a population analysis.

[14] Quoted in Milton M. Klein, ''New York in the American Colonies: A New Look,'' in Jacob Judd and Irwin Polishook, eds., *Aspects of Early New York Society and Politics* (Tarrytown, N.Y., 1973), p. 28.

[15] I have used the terms ''new social history'' and ''new political history'' reluctantly. They exaggerate the novelty of the demographic and quantitative research done in recent years, but they remain the best brief way to refer to these studies.

Cognizant of the importance of economic factors, though doubtful of their primacy, the study incorporates examinations of the distribution of wealth and of the role of commerce. Finally, it follows the lead of nineteenth century political historians in attempting to identify the reasons for the voters' responses to public issues.

A great variety of sources form the basis for the investigation: assessment and census rolls, church records, marriage licenses, genealogies, freemanship lists, indentures of apprenticeship, wills, inventories of estates, deeds, minutes of the courts, customhouse reports, journals of legislative assemblies and of executive councils, and the minutes of the Common Council, which include poll lists. Each has its individual bias, but collectively they hold the story of the varied people whose lives are the history of the city.[16] These raw materials yield their secrets grudgingly, but ultimately they tell much about what took place in the city and how inhabitants of all stations interpreted events. Not only the elite and the socially deviant appear in these sources, but also the ordinary citizens whom historians cannot neglect if they are to claim mankind for their jurisdiction.

Examination of these documents reveals that New York in the latter part of the seventeenth century was a Dutch town experiencing the consequences of the English conquest of 1664. New York was having its first encounter with the difficulties of combining in its society men and women of varied European national and religious backgrounds. Learning to live in a community composed of diverse elements was as great a problem for men of the seventeenth century as for later generations, and not surprisingly, a process of conflict and assimilation affected

[16] The Essay on Sources and Methods discusses the use of these materials and where they are located. They are also listed under primary sources in the bibliography.

every phase of life and helped determine the divisions in the municipality's politics.

England's conquest of New York naturally altered the composition of the population. The take-over encouraged large numbers of the King's subjects to migrate there from England or from earlier colonial settlements in New England or on Long Island. Many French Protestants, or Huguenots, befriended by the authorities in England as enemies of the Sun King, Louis XIV, joined the influx to New York in the wake of the revocation of the Edict of Nantes in 1685. By the end of the seventeenth century the English and French still did not outnumber the Dutch in New York, but they accounted for approximately 40 percent of the city's residents.

English and French New Yorkers soon exerted influence in the city beyond the strength of their numbers. Peculiarities in their patterns of migration produced in their ranks an unusually large percentage of well-to-do persons. While the typical descendants of the Dutch founders of the port enjoyed only a modest existence as simple craftsmen, the English and French provided a major share of the municipality's leadership.

Merchants were the princes of colonial society, and the rise of the English to commercial dominance in New York exemplifies the process by which the victors eased the vanquished from control of the city. English businessmen enjoyed the fundamental advantages of knowledge of the established language and personal connections in the mother country. These gave them access to the prerequisites of success—agency relationships and sources of credit. A few wealthy Dutch managed to duplicate these ties and prosper, but the burghers normally could not even compete with Huguenot and Jewish New Yorkers who conducted trade through their countrymen and co-religionists living in England.

Every aspect of life in New York, even the patterns of residence, reflected the demographic and economic changes which were occurring. English and French citizens established addresses on fashionable new waterfront streets at the southeastern tip of the island, while descendents of the Dutch settlers found themselves relegated to equally new, but socially less desirable, locations uptown in the interior of the island. By the end of the century, the English and French formed a majority of the inhabitants of the wealthiest ward, while the Dutch accounted for four out of every five families in the poorest district.

Gradually, New York's English and French minority translated their wealth and their connections into political dominance. This development was to be expected, but the frustration it caused drew many Dutch residents in 1689 to Jacob Leisler's Rebellion, the colony's response to England's Glorious Revolution. The Dutch insurgents did not seek to restore the province to the Netherlands, but rather to protest their loss of power to the new local order—the English and those Dutch who had accommodated themselves to their rule.

The collapse of Leisler's Rebellion in 1691 insured the political superiority of the English and French, but the basis of factionalism remained. When the unexpected death of Governor Bellomont in 1701 momentarily threatened the political equilibrium of the city, ethnic background again proved to be the chief cause of political allegiance. Ultimately, the increasing numerical strength of the English and French and the deaths of those who could remember the halcyon days of Dutch rule resolved the crisis and brought to a conclusion the turbulent first chapter in the history of pluralism in New York City.

New York's experiences late in the seventeenth century have a significance beyond the history of a single city. They show how the heterogeneity of a community can involve ordinary citizens in the political process in a way which can transform deferential politics into democratic politics. Most important, the story calls attention to the need for further study of the middle colonies.

2 ❧ The People of New York City

New York City established its polyglot image early in the seventeenth century, but commentators saw little reason for glorifying the heterogeneity. In 1643, Father Isaac Jogues, a French Jesuit missionary who had been captured by the Mohawks, escaped and made his way to the island port of New Amsterdam. Besides Dutch Calvinists, he met a Polish Lutheran, an Irish Catholic, and a Portuguese Catholic who displayed an image of the Italian Jesuit Aloysius Gonzaga in her house. Jogues estimated that four or five hundred men of different sects and nations, speaking as many as eighteen distinct languages, inhabited the town. "The arrogance of Babel," Jogues commented, "has done much harm to all men; the confusion of tongues has deprived them of great benefit." [1]

When England seized New Netherland in 1664, King Charles II renamed both the province and its capital New York in honor of the new proprietor, his younger brother James Stuart, Duke of York and heir apparent to the crown. The transfer of control added to the mixture of people, and Thomas Dongan, who arrived in 1683 as the new governor, must have muttered "Amen" to Father Jogues's evaluation. Four years later fascination and dismay permeated his report to the Committee of

[1] "Novum Belgium, by Father Isaac Jogues, 1646;" "Letter and Narrative of Father Isaac Jogues, 1643, 1645," J. Franklin Jameson, ed., *Narratives of New Netherland, 1609–1664* (New York, 1909), pp. 253, 259.

Trade and Plantations; ministers representing the Anglican, Huguenot, Dutch Calvinist, and Dutch Lutheran churches all served the faithful on Manhattan Island. The multiplicity of sects exasperated the governor, who evidently doubted the beneficial effects of such diversity: "Here bee not many of the Church of England; few Roman Catholicks; abundance of Quakers preachers men and Women especially; Singing Quakers; Ranting Quakers; Sabbatarians; Antisabbatarians; Some Anabaptists some Independants; some Jews; in short of all sorts of opinions there are some and the most part of none at all." [2]

The disillusionment expressed by Jogues and Dongan, who were accustomed to the more homogeneous nations of Europe, is understandable, but the composition of New York was not so variegated as their comments suggest. During the seventeenth century five ethnic and racial groups established themselves as the base of the population. The Dutch founded the city, and African, Jewish, English, and French immigrants soon joined them.

In 1621 the States General of the Netherlands had established the Dutch West India Company and granted it a trading monopoly and the right to establish colonies in the New World. Inspired by the voyage of Henry Hudson, an Englishman in service to the Dutch East India Company who in 1609 became the first European to explore closely the site of present-day New York, the West India Company chose Manhattan as the center of its proposed New Netherland Colony. In May 1626 the island welcomed its first significant influx of permanent white settlers, including the Walloon Peter Minuit, who purchased the land from the Manhates for 60 Dutch guilders.

[2] "Commission of Colonel Thomas Dongan to be Governor of New York," Sept. 30, 1682; "Governor Dongan's Report on the State of the Province," Feb. 22, 1687, *DRNY*, III, 328–29, 415.

Africans were added to New Amsterdam's population in 1626, when the Dutch West India Company imported eleven male slaves to work on projects which could not attract free labor. The Company throughout its tenure in New Netherland continued to purchase blacks in order to meet its labor needs. In 1648, hoping to stimulate the economies of two of its possessions, the Company relaxed its monopoly of the slave trade and authorized the citizens of New Netherland to send their produce to Brazil in return for blacks. Four years later, the Company legalized direct trade in slaves between New Netherland and Angola, but the African colony never became a popular source. Like other North Americans, the Dutch preferred to buy Africans who had already become acclimated to servitude, rather than more unruly recent captives. After the Portuguese captured Brazil in 1654, Curaçao, the Dutch island colony off the coast of South America, became the primary supplier of New Netherland's slaves. No exact figures remain to tell how many blacks were brought to New Netherland, but fragmentary statistics suggest that the number was large. Indeed, in 1664, the final year of Dutch control, a single ship, the *Gideon,* brought about three hundred slaves to the province, a number equal to 4 percent of the population.[3]

Spanish and Portuguese Jews, coming by a circuitous route through South America, made their initial appearance in New Amsterdam in the 1650s. At the end of the sixteenth century, large numbers of Marranos, or Jews who outwardly accepted Christianity while secretly practicing their old faith, had escaped from the Iberian peninsula to the Netherlands. From there many migrated to Pernambuco, the capital of Dutch Brazil, where

[3] Edmund B. O'Callaghan, ed., *Voyages of the Slavers "St. John" and "Arms of Amsterdam," 1659 and 1663* (Albany, 1867), intro.; Edgar J. McManus, *A History of Negro Slavery in New York* (Syracuse, N.Y., 1966), pp. 4–6, 11.

they built a prosperous settlement. However, when the Portuguese conquered the colony, they warned the Jews to leave within three months or face persecution as foreigners and heretics.[4]

Sixteen ships set sail for the Netherlands but Spanish pirates captured one of them. Fortunately, an armed French vessel, the *St. Charles,* rescued the victims, and its master, Jacques de la Motthe, offered to bring them to New Amsterdam for the price of 2500 guilders. When the twenty-three refugees reached the port in the first week of September, Governor Peter Stuyvesant, who deemed Jews usurious and deceitful, asked the West India Company for permission to deport them. But the Amsterdam Chamber of the company, cognizant of the sizable amount of capital invested in the organization by Dutch Jews, rejected his request and ordered him to allow the recent arrivals to settle and to trade.[5]

Immigrants from the Netherlands came to Manhattan in growing numbers as the years passed, and by 1652 the residents of New Amsterdam had developed sufficient economic and political strength to win from the Dutch West India Company a grant of incorporation. The director-general and council of the company appointed two burgomasters, five schepens, and a shout or sheriff, who took on both judicial and administrative responsibilities. New Amsterdam's burghers were not fully satisfied, because the company retained much influence, but they had taken the first steps toward municipal autonomy.

New Amsterdam in 1660 was a potentially thriving city. The Netherlands took pride in the port, and England, whose own

[4] Henry H. Kessler and Eugene Rachlis, *Peter Stuyvesant and His New York* (New York, 1959), pp. 176–77; David de Sola Pool, *Portraits Etched in Stone: Early Jewish Settlers, 1682–1831* (New York, 1952), pp. 4–5.

[5] Pool, *Portraits Etched in Stone,* p. 6; Harold C. Syrett, "Private Enterprise in New Amsterdam," *WMQ,* XI (Oct. 1954), 536–50.

possessions flanked it, felt envy. Throughout New Netherland's existence, the English claimed the territory by virtue of Henry Hudson's birth in their realm. New Englanders gave these assertions substance by establishing a number of settlements on nearby Long Island. Stuyvesant recognized the impossibility of forcing these populous towns to acknowledge allegiance to Holland or to the West India Company, and decided to protect the remaining lands in his domain by negotiating a clear boundary. By the Treaty of Hartford in 1650, New Netherland and Connecticut agreed to a line of demarcation on the mainland from Greenwich north, and on Long Island from Oyster Bay south to the Atlantic Ocean. The Dutch retained the territory to the west of the division, and the English received the area to the east.[6]

Oliver Cromwell's Puritan regime further weakened the Netherlands position in America by a legislative assault on the Dutch merchant fleet which controlled more than half of the carrying trade with the New World. The Navigation Act of 1651 required that the owner, master, and a majority of the crew of any ship bearing exports from England's colonial possessions be English, and similarly restricted the right of importation. In 1652 the Commonwealth went to war with the Dutch, partly over these laws, but a peace settlement in 1654 put an end to English plans to seize New Amsterdam.[7]

After his restoration in 1660, Charles II brought to fruition English hopes of establishing hegemony on the American mainland between Massachusetts and Virginia. On April 23, 1664, he commissioned Colonel Richard Nicolls, Sir Robert Carr, George Cartwright, and Samuel Maverick to reduce "the Dutch

---

[6] "Extract from the Despatch of Petrus Stuyvesant . . . to the Chamber of the West India Company at Amsterdam, dated 26th November, 1650," *DRNY*, I, 548.

[7] Lawrence A. Harper, *The English Navigation Laws* (New York, 1939), ch. 4; "Memorandum by Captain Bredon," Aug. 1678, *DRNY*, III, 270.

in or neare Long Island or any where within ye limits of our owne dominions to an entire obedience to our government.'' The king then promised his brother James jurisdiction over the territory ''from the west side of the Connecticutte River to the East Side of De La Ware Bay.'' [8]

By August 28, four English frigates bearing soldiers arrived in the offshore waters, and on September 4, six emissaries rowed to Manhattan to demand surrender of the colony. The negotiators promised to preserve the privileges of the inhabitants, and delivered an outline of their conditions to the governor. Stuyvesant tore up the letter, but the burghers forced him to piece it together again. Satisfied with the English offer, the townsmen refused to take up arms to defend the city, and Stuyvesant reluctantly struck the Dutch colors on September 5.[9]

By the Treaty of Breda in 1667 the Netherlands formally surrendered its claim to New York, but Amsterdam gained a measure of revenge when the Third Anglo-Dutch War erupted in 1673. On August 9 a fleet from the Netherlands, under Commanders Cornelius Evertse, Jr., and Jacob Benckes, sailed into New York harbor with several captured English ships in tow. The warships fired a broadside at the city's fort, and then landed troops on the island after the defenders returned the salvo. The English quickly struck their colors, and the town received its third European name, New Orange.[10]

---

[8] ''Instructions to the King's Commissioners to Massachusetts,'' Apr. 22, 1664; ''Grant of New Netherland . . . to the Duke of York,'' Mar. 12, 1664, *DRNY,* III, 51–52; II, 295–99.

[9] ''Answer of Ex-Director Stuyvesant . . . 1666;'' ''Extract of a Letter from the Director-General . . . to the Directors of the West India Company, Chamber at Amsterdam, dated the 4th of August, 1664;'' ''Director Stuyvesant to the Dutch Towns on Long Island,'' Aug. 28, 1664; ''Answer [of the Dutch Towns],'' n.d., *ibid.,* II, 431, 433, 444–45, 505, 376.

[10] ''Nathan Gould's Account of the Capture of New York,'' Aug. 1673, *ibid.,* III, 201.

Diplomatic considerations dictated that New Orange not remain under the jurisdiction of the Netherlands. The States General preferred peace to their New World colony, and offered Charles II a return to the *status quo ante bellum*. The king was receptive to the offer because continued Dutch control of the area constituted a severe threat to Virginia's shipping and offered New England's merchants too many temptations to engage in illicit trade. By the Treaty of Westminster in February 1674, England regained the territory; King Charles renamed the province and its port New York and placed it again under the jurisdiction of his brother James.[11]

Even as a Dutch town, though, New Amsterdam had attracted a handful of English settlers. John Haines was an active merchant in the port in 1646 and probably carried on business with his brother William, a Virginia resident who traded in the city. When John died around 1690, he left an estate which included £2.19.6 in silver objects. Thomas Willett, a native of Bristol, England, served as a soldier for the Dutch West India Company. In 1643 he married Sarah, the daughter of Thomas Comell, who had come from Essex and obtained land in the Bronx. Willett died early, and his widow married another Englishman, Charles Bridges of Canterbury. Sometime before 1639, Bridges had himself emigrated to the Dutch colony of Curaçao and changed his name to Van Brugge. He became a favorite of the island's director Peter Stuyvesant and accompanied him to New Amsterdam in 1647 when Stuyvesant took control of that settlement. Van Brugge, who restored his name to its original form after the English conquest, became a patentee of Flushing, on western Long Island, where he died in 1682.[12]

---

[11] "The States-General to Charles II," Dec. 19, 1673; "Report of the Council of Trade . . . respecting the Recapture of New York," Nov. 15, 1673, *ibid.,* II, 531; III, 211–13.

[12] Kenneth Scott, comp., *Gold and Silver in 17th Century New York Inventories* (New York, 1966), p. 12; J. H. Innes, *New Amsterdam and Its People* (New York, 1902), pp. 192–95.

After 1664, Englishmen came to New York in increasing numbers, but more than a decade after the conquest they accounted for less than one-fifth of the city's population. In 1677 the Common Council levied a tax for paying municipal expenses and recorded the assessments of approximately two hundred ninety heads of families.[13] Classification of the 275 ethnically recognizable names shows that 218 or 79.3 percent were Dutch, 51 or 18.5 percent were English, and 6 or 2.2 percent were French or Jewish.

Though many occupations had no recognizable English representative, the newcomers were engaged in a variety of endeavors. Samuel Leete was clerk of the Mayor's Court. According to deeds in which they were later involved or mentioned, John Reay was a pipemaker and Richard Tinker a laborer. John Watkins was one of the carmen or carters who moved goods through the city.[14]

English immigrants made their biggest mark in the 1670s as merchants, though. John Darvall came to New York from Boston in 1667 and accumulated an estate estimated at £3000 in 1676. John Lawrence had come to Long Island during the reign of Charles I; he converted his commercial abilities into political prominence and served as mayor of New York City in 1671 and 1691. Robert Story had two houses and an estate worth £1000 in 1676; when he died in 1683 he left to his wife, Patience, and children, Enoch and Mercy, valuables which included £101.18.0 worth of gold and silver items. Samuel Wilson, who came to the port in the wake of the English take-over, served as the town's surveyor and by 1676 accumulated an estate worth £2500.[15]

[13] *Min. Com. Coun.*, July 24, 1677, I, 50–62.

[14] *Ibid.*, Oct. 13, 1675, pp. 4–5, 73; Con. Lib., Mar. 24, 1687, XVIII, 53–55, Jan. 9, 1683, XIII, 57–58.

[15] David T. Valentine, *History of the City of New York* (New York, 1853), pp. 76, 233, 246; *Min. Com. Coun.*, Apr. 18 and Nov. 10, 1676, I, 14, 33–34.

The success of Englishmen as merchants was a portent of New York's future, but the Dutch still dominated the city in 1677. Active in every trade, the burghers more than held their own. John Hendricks De Bruyn had one of the very highest assessments in 1677, as did Nicholas De Meyer who paid taxes on a "little house" and a "great new house" as well as on his residence. Oloff Stevensen Van Cortlandt, who came to New Amsterdam in 1637 as a soldier and became an important merchant, had an assessment of £3000 in 1676, and Frederick Philipse, whose son married Van Cortlandt's daughter Catharina in 1692, had paid taxes on £13,000, the largest estate in New York.[16]

In terms of total wealth, too, New York remained a Dutch city in the 1670s. One can compare the relative wealth of the two groups by arranging the 269 Dutch and English names on the 1677 tax rolls according to the size of their assessment and then dividing this list into four "intervals" or categories of relatively equal size.[17] The English had more representation than might be expected in the highest interval, but in general the Dutch achieved in each bracket a dominance proportionate to their numbers in the general population (Table 1).

Manhattan's English population continued to grow in the late seventeenth century, but government officials despaired at the

[16] Con. Lib., Feb. 15, 1686, XIII, 193–95; *Min. Com. Coun.*, Nov. 10, 1676, July 24, 1677, I, 31–33, 51, 56; Valentine, *History of New York*, p. 79; Innes, *New Amsterdam*, pp. 75–78; Edwin Ruthven Purple, *Genealogical Notes Relating to Lieut.-Gov. Jacob Leisler and His Family Connections in New York* (New York, 1877), p. 17.

[17] The distribution pattern of assessments on the 1677 tax lists made it impossible to include an equal number of people in each of the four intervals. This also prohibited division into five equal intervals, which would have facilitated comparisons with data based on five- and ten-interval scales later in this chapter. For an explanation see the Essay on Sources and Methods. Also note that throughout the study, the category "Dutch" includes a few Dutch-speakers of other nations; "English" includes all the British Isles.

Table 1. Percentage of the major nationality groups in each division of the four-interval scale of wealth for 1677 and the five-interval scale of wealth for 1703

Year	Size of population	Percentage of population	Percentage of interval				
			High	4th	3rd	2nd	Low
1677							
Dutch	218	81	77	n.a.	82	83	84
English	51	19	23	n.a.	18	17	16
Total	269						
1703							
Dutch	372	58.5	47	63	62.5	67	52
English/French	263	41.5	53	37	37.5	33	48
Total	635						
Dutch	393	55	46	62	59	61	46
English/French	322	45	54	38	41	39	54
Total	715						
Dutch	474	56	52	59	64	63	44
English/French	367	44	48	41	36	37	56
Total	841						

Sources: The 1677 and 1703 assessment lists, conveyance libers, church and court records, freemanship rolls, genealogies, and others mentioned previously

slow rate. Thomas Dongan complained that the king's subjects avoided New York in favor of neighboring colonies where reasonably priced land was more available. The governor made evident his pessimism in a 1687 report that "for these last 7 years past, there has not come into this province twenty English, Scotch or Irish families." [18]

In fact, Dutch New Yorkers might have been able to maintain their superiority in the city had it not been for the addition to the population in the late seventeenth century of many French Protestant refugees, who resembled the English socially and followed their lead politically. These refugees joined a contingent of other Huguenots who had been among the first settlers dispatched to Manhattan by the Dutch West India Company. The early arrivals were descendants of Protestants who had emigrated to the Netherlands during the years of religious warfare

[18] "Governor Dongan's Report on the State of the Province," Feb. 22, 1687, *DRNY,* III, 399.

that followed the St. Bartholomew's Day Massacre of 1572. Among them were the forebears of Peter Minuit, the first director-general of New Netherland, who had fled to the Dutch town of Wesel. The Reverend Balthazar Bayard abandoned a professorship at the Protestant University of Paris during the reign of Louis XIII, and his son Samuel became the brother-in-law of Peter Stuyvesant and the progenitor of one of New York's most important families.[19]

The major migration of Huguenots to America began in the latter part of the seventeenth century when Louis XIV, who equated heterodoxy with treason, renewed large-scale persecution of the Protestants in his kingdom. In 1685 the Sun King, who incorrectly believed that few heretics remained in his dominion, set off an exodus of about two hundred thousand Huguenots from France by revoking the Edict of Nantes. Many of the refugees went temporarily to England and then proceeded to the American colonies. They migrated most frequently to South Carolina and New York, where they established the town of New Rochelle in present Westchester County and formed the second wave of French immigrants to Manhattan Island.[20]

Merchants from the important French seaport of La Rochelle, its neighboring province Aunis, and the nearby Isle of Ré were the most prominent Huguenot arrivals in New York. These men had been active in trade and in the construction and outfitting of ships, and had even insured the ventures undertaken in their vessels. Augustus Jay of La Rochelle, the son of a Huguenot merchant and grandfather of the American Founding Father

---

[19] Charles W. Baird, *History of the Huguenot Emigration to America* (New York, 1885; reprinted Baltimore, 1966), I, 175; [Mrs.] Anson Phelps Atterbury, *The Bayard Family* (Baltimore, 1928), p. 28; Martha J. Lamb, "The Career and Times of Nicholas Bayard," *Proceedings of the Huguenot Society of America*, II (1888–1891), 31–32, 36.

[20] "Petition of the French Protestants of New York," May 1687, *DRNY*, III, 419.

John Jay, settled in Manhattan in this period. The Faneuil family of New York and Boston, which had owned six ships totaling 670 tons in La Rochelle, also came to America during these years.[21]

As Dutch, English, French, and Jewish whites combined to swell the city's population, they increased the market for slaves, a commodity which the colony's proprietor, a patron of the Royal African Company, was quite willing to supply. In contrast with the Dutch West India Company, which had used slavery to implement colonial policy, James Stuart and the Royal African Company used New York to foster slavery. By the end of the seventeenth century, trading in human lives had become a staple of the province's economy. In 1698 the merchant Jacobus Van Cortlandt had to advise Miles Mayhew, a West Indian client, that the large stock of available blacks made it impossible to sell any slave over twenty-five years of age.[22]

At the end of the seventeenth century Dutch, English, French, Jews, and Africans composed the vast majority of New York's population. Original tax assessment rolls compiled in 1703 and a census taken in the same year show clearly the numerical balance and the relative economic well-being of these groups. In addition to names, these lists provide the estimated value of the estate and the number of bondsmen and dependents for the city's householders and tenants. A group of 876 of these persons for whom sufficient biographical information was available became the population examined in this book. They accounted for a high percentage of all the independent residents or

[21] Baird, *Huguenot Emigration,* I, 263–64, 302; M. P. Boissonade, ''La Marine marchande, le port et les armateurs de la Rochelle à l'époque de Colbert, 1662–1683,'' *Bulletin de la section de géographie: Comité de travaux historiques et scientifiques,* XXXVII (1922), 29, 43–44.

[22] McManus, *Negro Slavery,* p. 23; Van Cortlandt to Mayhew, July 16, 1698, Jacobus Van Cortlandt Letter Book, 1698–1700, New-York Historical Society.

heads of families in Manhattan's five central wards, the East, West, North, South, and Dock.[23]

Determining the national backgrounds of the 876 persons under examination was a task filled with problems. The Dutch, English, and French languages have many surnames, such as Jansen or Johnson, Roberts, and Smith, which are similar or the same. Under the lax orthographic standards of the seventeenth and eighteenth centuries little effort was made to distinguish between them. Moreover, the assessors and census takers understandably were flustered by the city's Babylon of names. Trying as best they could to transcribe the strange sounds, English officials often anglicized. A few examples show how Dutch names evolved into English ones: Marius became Morris; Pels, Pell; and Roos, Rose.

Prudence demanded that nationalities be assigned to individuals only on the basis of evidence beyond a rudimentary analysis of surnames. Thorough mining of primary and secondary sources made possible positive identification of the ethnic backgrounds of 650 adult males. Of those individuals not categorized, 136 were women, the vast majority of whom were widows whose own heritage was hidden behind the surnames of their deceased husbands.

The 650 adult males, and especially the 638 of them who were Dutch, English, or French, became the focus of this analysis. To be certain this method of selection did not introduce a bias into the study, supplemental calculations were made on a group of 194 additional men and women who had previously been rejected. They were assigned nationalities after a cautious examination of surnames. The 194 persons added to the original

[23] New York City, Assessment Rolls, 1703–1704, microfilm, Klapper Library, Queens College, City University of New York; "Census of the City of New York [About the Year 1703]," *DHNY*, I, 611–24. The Essay on Sources and Methods discusses more fully the materials used.

650 made a total of 844 individuals to whom nationalities were at least tentatively ascribed, out of the base population of 876. Computations performed on both sets of data confirmed one another, and the information derived from the larger body revealed some interesting details.

Four decades after the fall of New Amsterdam, the Dutch remained the most numerous contingent in Manhattan's population. The birth and marriage records of the Reformed Church and an occasional genealogy provide proof that 374 individuals or heads of families shared Dutch ancestry. Their portion of the population, which was almost twice as large as the English segment, included 43 percent of the total group of 876 and 58 percent of the 650 persons whose nationalities were positively identified.[24]

English and French newcomers accounted for approximately 40 percent of the Manhattanites whose nationalities have been determined. The minutes of Trinity Church, the Anglican house of worship in Manhattan, and other documents indicate that at the opening of the eighteenth century, 190 of the people under scrutiny were of Anglo-Saxon or Celtic stock; they accounted for 22 percent of the test population and 29 percent of the ethnically identifiable group. Seventy-four individuals or heads of families in 1703, distinguished primarily from the records of the Eglise du Saint-Esprit, had their roots in France; they constituted 8 percent of the test group and 11 percent of its ethnically recognizable portion.[25]

Only 12 of the 876 names under examination were Jewish. In 1682, the group obtained a cemetery, which today is nestled among the buildings of Chatham Square in lower Manhattan, but forty-six years passed before tombstones filled the 54-foot by 52-foot plot. This tiny band of people, accounting for

[24] *Coll. NYGBS,* Vols. II and IX.   [25] Min. Ves.; *Coll. HSA.*

slightly less than 2 percent of the total white population in 1703, represented the first of the migrations which would eventually make New York City the home of the largest Jewish community in the world.[26]

Including in the calculations those persons assigned nationalities on the basis of surnames alone affects the distribution only slightly. Of the 638 Dutch, English, and French positively identified, the first group accounted for 58.6 percent, the second for 29.7 percent, and the third for 11.7 percent. On the basis of the larger set of 844, the Dutch totaled 56.3 percent, the English 32.6 percent, and the French 11.1 percent, or 476, 275, and 93 respectively.

Blacks composed as much as 20 percent of New York's population in 1703. The few who were free usually lived on the farm lands north of the city's central wards and only occasionally appear in the records. On November 18, 1691, for example, Pieter Lucaszen and Maryken Jans were married, and a few weeks later, the widower Francis Bastiaenszen and the widow Anna Mary Van Curaçao were also wed.[27]

Most blacks, however, spent their lives in bondage, a silent minority exploited and feared by their masters. The census of 1703 contains evidence concerning slave ownership for 537 of the 876 whites under scrutiny. It shows that at least 233 or 43 percent of the group held bondsmen. Although the percentage of families or individuals owning slaves was high, especially when compared with the 6.6 percent estimate made recently for Philadelphia in the same era, the number of blacks in each household was usually low. O'Callaghan's 1703 census contains a total of

[26] Pool, *Portraits Etched in Stone,* p. 5. The number of Jews is underestimated because the sources occasionally identify them solely by such obscure notations as "Jacob ye Jew."

[27] *Coll. NYGBS,* IX, 71.

306 slaveowners who held a total of 692 slaves, for an average of 2.26 per family. In addition, as many as 139 of the masters kept only one bondsman.[28]

Slaves by definition formed the economic bottom of New York's society. Most served their masters primarily as domestic help. Females were as numerous as males, and a majority of those families which owned only one slave owned a woman. Females appear more frequently than males even in the 79 households which kept two Negroes; in only 11 of these homes were both slaves male, whereas in 22 both were women. Members of no particular occupational or professional group owned a disproportionately large percentage of blacks. The owners often could have had little use for slaves other than as household help or personal servants. For example, 15 gentlemen, whose title recognized their high social status, owned 26 bondsmen, and 76 widows an additional 83. The widows may have inherited the slaves from their husbands and probably would have found them most useful as laborers around their lodgings.

New York's whites uniformly fared better than its slaves, but clear social and economic distinctions separated the various European elements of the population as well. Young Dutch men and women did not frequently find spouses among the English and French newcomers. The records of the Reformed Church do not show a single instance of Dutch union with outsiders in the approximately one hundred New York City weddings performed in 1675, 1676, and 1678–1681. The frequency of intermarriage increased slightly in the 1680s. One of the most interesting cases, in light of later events, occurred in 1685, when a leading Dutch merchant Jacob Leisler gave his daughter Catharina to

[28] Gary B. Nash, "Slaves and Slaveowners in Colonial Philadelphia," *WMQ*, XXX (Apr. 1973), 226; "Census of the City of New York."

Robert Walters, a native of Plymouth, England. The rate of intermarriage rose sharply for a brief period in the 1690s but had dropped again by the end of the century.[29]

French New Yorkers also married primarily within their own group. Not a single one of the 44 weddings which took place in the Eglise du Saint-Esprit between 1689 and 1710 involved a non-French person. Nevertheless, the French developed close ties with the English. They were grateful for the generosity of the English government, which offered invaluable assistance to the exiles, including giving aid for the emigrants to America and maintenance of many indigent Huguenots in London. French merchants also shared common interests with their English counterparts, and the ambitious among the exiles soon realized that the owners of the colony controlled the access to power. Moreover, for a variety of reasons, the Huguenots in New York, like most of those elsewhere in the colonies, did not pattern their ecclesiastical organization after the Dutch Reformed Church, with which they shared Calvinist principles, but rather followed the Anglican example.[30]

By 1703 the English and their French associates had replaced the Dutch as the dominant group in New York. The descendants of the founders of New Amsterdam clustered in less prestigious professions and enjoyed less prosperous lives than many of their English and French townsmen who had more recently come to the port. The Dutch were still the most numerous group in New York, but the size of their majority had decreased significantly since 1677, and more important, by 1703 they accounted for only a minority of the wealthiest citizens.

[29] *Coll. NYGBS,* IX, 39–50, 56. The reasons for the erratic patterns of the 1690s are properly the concern of Chapter 6.

[30] Robert M. Kingdon, ''Pourquoi les réfugiés huguenots aux colonies américaines, sont-ils devenus épiscopaliens?'' *Bulletin de al Société de l'Histoire du Protestaintisme Français,* XLII (October-November-December 1969), 504–9.

Arranging the names on the 1703 assessment rolls in order of the size of their estates and dividing this ranking into five and ten intervals created two scales similar to the one devised earlier for the 1677 tax list. Each person in the test population was then assigned a score corresponding to his or her position on the ten-interval scale. The scales and scores make it possible to compute the average and median wealth of the Dutch, English, and French citizens and to determine the intragroup distributions along the scales. And, analysis of the relative representation of the Dutch, English, and French at the various levels of the scales illustrates with some precision the comparative economic well-being of the three major white components of the island's population at the beginning of the eighteenth century.[31]

Of the 638 persons identified with certainty as being Dutch, English or French, assessments were available for 635. Examination of these reveals that the English were emerging as the most affluent group in the city. Manhattan's average English inhabitant in 1703 scored 6.1 points on the ten-interval scale and his Dutch neighbor 5.5. When median standings become the criteria, the English again emerge as the most well-to-do. Fully half of the English contingent ranked in the seventh or an even higher interval, whereas the Dutch mid-point was in the sixth bracket.

French New Yorkers scored an average of only 5.0 and their median point was in the fifth bracket. Overrepresentation in the highest and lowest categories, a result of the greater likelihood of the rich and poor to become émigrés, explains their poor showing and testifies to the broad compass and thorough application of Louis XIV's program to discourage heresy. Many Huguenots, whatever their former station, escaped with nothing save their lives, and suffered great deprivations in exile;

---

[31] The Essay on Sources and Methods discusses this procedure in greater detail.

hundreds of them received continuous mention on the London public assistance rolls.[32] The most fortunate, like the Faneuils and the Jays, were able to transfer their wealth and influence to new homes in America. Doubtless many Huguenots of middle station, too affluent to move as freely as the poor but not rich enough to have liquid assets, decided to risk persecution rather than emigrate.

Expansion of the group under scrutiny to include the additional 194 citizens tentatively identified as Dutch, English or French modifies the picture of economic stratification somewhat. Average wealth declined for all three groups. The English score fell from 6.0 to 5.39, the Dutch from 5.5 to 5.49, and the French from 5.0 to 4.80. In terms of median standing, the English ranked in the sixth rather than the seventh interval, the French in the fourth rather than the fifth interval, while the Dutch remained in the sixth.

The findings suggest two conclusions. Among the residents of the city at the beginning of the eighteenth century who were firmly enough established to leave more than minimal traces of their existence, the English had become the economically dominant group. The sizable decline in the average wealth of the English which occurred when the larger base figure was used was the consequence of and evidence of the continuing influx into New York of English citizens, some of whom were transients or not long enough established to gain either fortune or recognition in the records.

Collapsing the original ten intervals of the scale into five shows more clearly the nature of New York City's economic stratification at the end of the seventeenth century. With the

[32] City of London, Account of the Distribution Made to the Poor French Protestant Refugees, of the Money Proceeding Both from the Subscriptions and of the Collection Granted by the King's Most Excellent Majesty, the 31st March 1694. Guildhall Library, London.

core group of 635 used as the basis for calculation, a larger percentage of the English ranked in the highest category than in any other. The Dutch gravitated toward the central ranges and appeared least frequently in the lowest and highest intervals, a natural phenomenon under conditions of normal distribution. Finally, the French concentrated in the lowest and highest brackets, having 31 percent of their number at the bottom of the scale and 28 percent, fully as large a percentage as the English, at the top (Table 2).

Table 2. Distribution of Dutch, English, and French on the five-interval scale of wealth for 1703

Nationality	Size of population	Percentage in interval				
		High	4th	Middle	2nd	Low
Dutch	372	17	23	19	26	15
English	189	28	24	16	18	14
French	74	28	8	15	18	31
Total	635					
Dutch	393	17	24	18	25	16
English	239	23	21	16	20	20
French	83	26	8	14	21	31
Total	715					
Dutch	474	19	21	19	26	15
English	274	21	22	15	20	22
French	93	26	9	13	20	32
Total	841					

Sources: The 1703 assessment list and others mentioned previously

Oldtimers and newcomers to New York mixed in the lowest bracket of the five-internal scale of wealth and in the least lucrative occupations and social groups. The Dutch, who accounted for 58 percent of the population under examination, contributed only 52 percent to the bottom economic group, but had 57 of the 88 residents who followed the seven least remunerative employments. In this group, the Dutch were especially active as carmen or carters, the English as victuallers or innkeepers, and the French as shipwrights. The Dutch had more than twice the representation of the English and the French in the nine middle-ranking employments.[33] They outnumbered their neighbors by 9 to 0 as blacksmiths, by 26 to 11 as carpenters, by 17 to 4 as coopers, or cask and barrel makers, by 33 to 4 as cordwainers, or shoemakers and leatherworkers, by 6 to 0 as silversmiths, and by 4 to 1 as yeomen (Table 3).

Employment in these less prestigious pursuits did not make the acquisition of wealth impossible. Ability, ambition, social connections, and participation in commercial activities beyond the narrow limits of their callings brought some skilled and

Table 3. Median economic standing, on a ten-interval scale, and ethnic breakdown of the largest social and occupational groups in 1703

Group	Members	Median standing	Dutch	English	French	Jewish	Unknown
Merchant	110	9	36	29	31	8	6
Bolter	13	8	12	0	1	0	0
Goldsmith	7	8	3	2	0	0	2
Gentleman	26	7	4	2	4	0	1
Baker	24	7	15	7	0	0	2
Master	55	6	18	21	4	0	12
Cordwainer	38	6	33	3	1	0	1
Silversmith	7	6	6	0	0	0	1
Yeoman	5	6	4	1	0	0	0
Blacksmith	12	5/6	9	0	0	0	3
Widow	136	5	77	33	9	2	15
Carpenter	41	5	26	10	1	0	4
Mariner	31	5	14	9	4	0	4
Cooper	24	5	17	2	2	0	3
Tailor	10	4/6	5	3	2	0	0
Victualler	20	4/5	6	9	3	0	2
Chirurgeon	8	4/5	6	2	0	0	0
Shipwright	21	4	7	8	4	0	2
Carman	13	4	11	1	0	0	1
Butcher	9	4	2	3	0	1	1
Brickmaker	24	3/4	14	3	3	0	4
Bellringer	7	3	5	1	0	0	1

Sources: The 1703 assessment list and others mentioned previously

[33] Women not included in this analysis.

unskilled workers economic success beyond that of their occupational peers. Some also acted as shopkeepers or retailers. Samuel Mynderts, a Dutch glover who scored 8.0 on the ten-interval scale of individual financial standing, produced leather goods and maintained a store. The inventory of estate taken at the time of Mynderts's death in 1702 shows that he possessed not only three score pairs of gloves, hundreds of animal skins, and his tools, but that he also had a variety of non-leather merchandise. Listed in the inventory were 21 ivory combs, 15 pairs of spectacles, yards of silk, calico, and other cloths, and an assortment of books, including seven dozen catechisms and four dozen alphabet primers.[34] Perhaps Mynderts's willingness and ability to diversify was the factor which gave him an economic standing several positions higher than that enjoyed by the typical New York cordwainer.

Many of the Dutch who made the top rank held key positions in New York's important flour trade and in the production of the city's food; in those cases in which national identities have been determined, they contributed 12 of the 13 bolters or processors of flour, and 15 of the 22 bakers. They also accounted for 3 of the 5 goldsmiths whose nationalities are known. Goldsmiths like David Lyell, who became the city's sealer and maker of weights and measures in 1709, and Jacob Boelen, who won election four times as alderman of the North Ward, may properly be included among the more important residents of the city. In the colonial era possession of even small amounts of precious metals was evidence of wealth and high social status (Table 3).[35]

Access to real wealth lay in the professions and prestigious social positions in which English and French influence was

[34] Inventory of the estate of Samuel Mynderts, 1702, Klapper Library.

[35] Minutes of the Court of Quarter Sessions, May 3, 1709, Criminal Court Building, New York, p. 159; *Min. Com. Coun.,* Sept 29, 1695, 1697, 1698, I, 381; II, 14, 56.

strongest. Although they accounted for only 42 percent of the population under examination, English and French citizens outnumbered the Dutch 76 to 70 in the five leading occupational classifications.

English and French dominance of New York is indicated by their claim to the titles of "gentleman" and "merchant." Gentlemen, who enjoyed their title by virtue of social eminence and political position, were by definition members of the elite. At least 21 representatives of the Anglo-French contingent were described in the records as gentlemen, but only 4 Dutch residents enjoyed that distinction. The merchants were the wealthiest group in the port. Although Dutch heads of families outnumbered their English and French counterparts by a margin of 110, only 36 Dutch acted as merchants while 60 English and French did (Table 3). Their prominence as merchants enabled the English and French, despite their minority position within the population, to include in their ranks 53 percent of the individuals in the highest bracket of the five-interval scale of wealth (Table 1).

Similar analyses based on two larger groups of New Yorkers confirm and elucidate the results derived from the core population of 635. In one set of calculations a selection of 841 persons whose nationalities could be at least tentatively determined and whose assessments were known became the focus. In the other, females were excluded due to lack of information about them, and a group of 715 underwent scrutiny.

The use of the larger base figures made only one notable change. The distribution of the Dutch and the French in the group of 841 remained virtually static, but the presence of a number of poorer English raised the percentage of that group in the lowest portion of the five-interval scale from 14 to 22 and lowered the percentage in the most affluent interval from 28 to 21 (Table 2). Of the additional 34 English persons found in the lowest economic category, 22 were males. Little can be discovered about them, but apparently most of them were young, perhaps recent arrivals who had yet to establish themselves. Of the 12 whose marriage status is known 4 were single, and of the 6 whose date of marriage is available, 3 were wed between 1691 and 1695, and 3 after 1695. At least 2 of the men had higher pretensions than their economic status indicated; Daniel Thwaits was a schoolmaster and Daniel Toy a gentleman.

Examination of the relative importance of the Dutch, English, and French on all three scales of wealth highlights a key trend in the distribution of wealth in Manhattan. The data confirms the importance of the long-established Dutch in the city's middle classes. It also suggests the wealth of the Dutch in 1703 was that of an older, declining element of the population. Regardless of the number of citizens under investigation, the Dutch never enjoyed representation in the top economic category equivalent to their numerical importance in the population. Only when women were included in the analysis, and money belonging to Dutch widows whose lingering wealth was a memento of an older social order came into play, did the Dutch proportion in the top bracket of the five-interval scale pass 50 percent (Table 1). Indeed, of the 23 persons in the highest economic bracket listed as of ''unknown nationality'' but tentatively identified as Dutch, 22 were women.

Evidence drawn from the analyses of the three groups of 635, 715, and 841 persons demonstrates that the English and the French had a disproportionately large presence in the ranks of New York's most affluent citizenry, and it further indicates that their wealth was that of a newer, ascending group. The finding is of major significance, because differences in economic standing were great in the city and a chasm separated the elite from their fellow citizens. In terms of the property assessments available for almost all the 876 persons who formed the test population, the approximately 20 percent in the lowest two categories

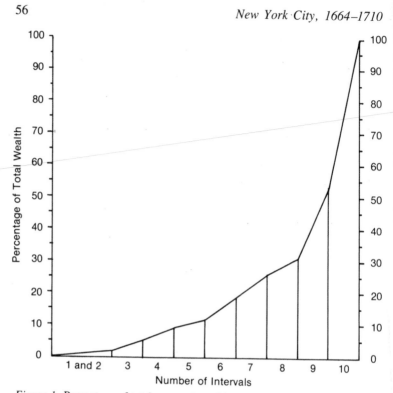

Figure 1. Percentage of total assessed wealth controlled by persons ranking in the various intervals of the ten-interval scale of wealth for 1703

of the ten-interval scale owned not even 3 percent of the city's total wealth (Figure 1). Theophilus Elsworth, a young shoemaker living with his father in 1703, represented the bottom rung of the financial ladder. Elsworth's fortunes apparently did not improve in the years before his early death in 1712, and his estate totaled only £23. The young man's most valuable possessions, besides fourteen hides "not quite tanned" (£4.10) which he used in his work, were his bed and its accessories (£3). His sole luxury was a "milch" cow (£2.10).[36]

[36] Inventory of the estate of Theophilus Elsworth, Klapper Library; Howard S. F. Randolph, "The Elsworth Family of New York with the Related Fami-

New Yorkers who ranked in the highest bracket of the ten-interval scale, including 40 English and French residents and 35 Dutch, controlled 47 percent of the city's taxable resources. The approximately 20 percent in the two highest brackets, of whom 53 percent were English and French, controlled 69 percent of the total assessments (Figure 1). Isaac Rodriques Marques, a merchant who ranked in the tenth interval, enjoyed an estate of £3400 at his death in 1703. Robert Skelton, a tailor whose assessment placed him in the sixth section of the ten-interval scale, had at his death in 1704 a £336 estate, only one-tenth the size of Marques's inventory.[37]

Assessments, inventories, and other indices of wealth can but palely reflect the great changes which occurred in New York City in the last quarter of the seventeenth century. To the average Dutch citizen, whose family probably had resided in Manhattan for at least a generation, the upper classes must have seemed unduly foreign and filled with late English and French arrivals. The Dutch no longer controlled New York City and the sounds of the voices conducting business along the wharves confirmed their loss.

---

lies of Rommen–Romme–Van Langstraat and Roome," *NYGB Rec.,* LXIV (Apr. 1933), 163.

[37] Inventories of the estates of Isaac Rodriques Marques and Robert Skelton, Klapper Library; Con. Lib., Feb. 28, 1704, XXV, 336–37; June 13, 1693, XVIII, 225–27.

3 ❦ The Merchants

Commerce has been the lifeblood of New York City from the time of its founding. Dreams of mercantile riches inspired the Antwerp merchant William Usselinx to establish a corporation in the New World to duplicate the success of the East India Company. Chartered by the States General in 1621, the Dutch West India Company founded New Amsterdam in 1625, and within a few years the settlers were sending back ships loaded with pelts and timber for use in shipbuilding.[1]

Ambitious young Dutchmen sought and sometimes found their fortunes as merchants in New Amsterdam throughout the period of the company's rule. Govert Loockermans arrived in 1633 as the assistant to a ship's cook, but soon earned a position as a clerk for the Dutch West India Company. Within a few years Loockermans became a trader, and by the time of his death in 1671 he was one of the leading merchants in the city. Loockermans's sister Anneken in 1642 married Oloff Stevensen Van Cortlandt, another young man who enjoyed spectacular success in the New World. Van Cortlandt came to New Amsterdam in 1637 as a soldier with the Dutch West India Company. He soon became commissary, or superintendent of cargoes, at the port, and after his marriage obtained appointment as keeper of the public store. Van Cortlandt eventually became a distin-

[1] "From the 'Historisch Verhael,' by Nicolaes Van Wassenaer, 1624–1630," J. Franklin Jameson, ed., *Narratives of New Netherland, 1609–1664* (New York, 1909), p. 87.

guished merchant and the progenitor of one of the colony's most important landholding and commercially active families.[2]

English merchants became prominent in New York soon after their country added the province to its web of colonies in 1664. Article 6 of the capitulation agreement stipulated that "any people may come here [New York] freely from the Netherlands and plant in this country, and that Dutch vessels may freely come hither, and any of the Dutch may freely return home, or send any sort of merchandise home in vessels of their own country." But the English government in 1668 forbade vessels from the Netherlands to bring their cargoes to Manhattan, and in any case no treaty could prevent London from replacing Amsterdam as the most important link in New York's commerce.[3]

The preponderance of Dutch among the wealthy inhabitants on the 1677 tax list suggests that the old burghers still controlled the city's commerce, but a significant minority of the merchants bore English names. Men like William Merritt, who served for three years as the city's mayor in the 1690s, and William Pinhorne, who later served on the Governor's Council, were building their fortunes on Manhattan's wharves, and in the next quarter century other Englishmen and a number of Huguenots joined them.[4] By 1703 the English and the French outnumbered the Dutch by 60 to 36 among the identified merchants (Table 3).

Few personal documents belonging to early New York mer-

---

[2] J. H. Innes, *New Amsterdam and Its People* (New York, 1902), pp. 75–78, 235–44.

[3] "Articles of Capitulation on the Reduction of New Netherland," Aug. 27, 1664; "Order in Council Prohibiting Dutch Ships to Trade to New York," Nov. 18, 1668, *DRNY*, II, 251; III, 177. There is evidence that some trade continued between Amsterdam and Albany, but New York City merchants apparently did not participate in these ventures. See Jan Kupp, "Aspects of New York–Dutch Trade under the English, 1670–1674," *New-York Historical Society Quarterly*, LVIII, (Apr. 1974), 141.

[4] David T. Valentine, *History of the City of New York* (New York, 1853), pp. 238–40.

chants have survived, but the customhouse records clearly show what kind of transformation had taken place in the city's merchant group during the last quarter of the seventeenth century.[5] Preserved in full for the years 1701 and 1702, and thus useful in conjunction with available tax and census materials, the documents help identify New York's merchant class and provide a good impression of the city's important patterns of trade. Careful study of these statistics show the extent to which English and French residents controlled the port's seaborne business and reveal the means by which they surpassed the Dutch.

The customhouse records divide commerce into four spheres of activity: the importation of general merchandise, of rum, and of wine, and the exportation of furs. Each entry identifies the merchant responsible for the shipment and notes the value of the cargo and the duties paid in the case of merchandise, or only the duties paid in the case of imported rum and wine and exported furs. Using these figures, we can construct four scales, similar to the ones used previously to estimate relative wealth, to measure the extent of activity by individual merchants in each category. A fifth scale, devised from the data on these four, can indicate relative overall commercial importance.[6]

English and French names appear more frequently than Dutch ones in almost every interval of the overall scale (Table 4). The newcomers have a numerical edge among the minor importers and exporters of the four lowest intervals, and the same advantage in the middle range, the fifth through seventh intervals. Most important, the English and French dominate the top three brackets, the eighth, ninth, and tenth, to an extent that clearly shows why they, and a few Dutch who managed to maintain

[5] *HMR*.

[6] The Essay on Sources and Methods discusses this procedure in more detail.

their positions under the new order, controlled New York. Their function not only made them the most prosperous group on the island but also gave them great influence in the management of the municipality and the colony.

Occasional traders are the mainstay of the overall scale's four lowest intervals, in which 25 English, 4 French, and 21 Dutch inhabitants are represented. Only rarely did a New Yorker who claimed the title "merchant" do so little business as to fall into this bottom range. These least active importers and exporters usually obtained products for their own use or engaged in small

Table 4. Members of major ethnic groups in each interval of the scale of commercial importance

Ethnic group	Intervals							
	10th	9th	8th	7th	6th	5th	3rd & 4th	1st & 2nd
Dutch	6	2	6	2	5	7	10	11
English	9	10	3	5	1	6	12	13
French	3	3	3	5	1	3	3	1
Jewish	1	1	2	4	0	1	1	0
Unknown	0	1	0	1	3	2	7	6

Sources: *HMR* and others mentioned previously

speculative ventures to supplement their main source of income. They pursued a variety of nonmercantile occupations, but most frequently identified themselves as masters, or ships' captains. Eight of the 25 nonmerchants in the third and fourth brackets and 10 of the 27 in the two lowest commanded vessels.

Masters engaged in commerce may often have been dealing in small parcels of trading goods given to them by merchants as primage to encourage the careful and expeditious handling of their cargoes. In some instances, however, the masters did not import or export in their own vessels. This latter pattern suggests that they were as much part-time shippers who used their special knowledge to make promising small investments as they were "merchants of opportunity" who only occasionally obtained items for trade.[7]

The presence of 12 English and 9 French inhabitants in the fifth, sixth, and seventh brackets gives the newcomers dominance in the middle range of the scale. Some of the persons in these intervals were wealthy individuals taking advantage of a speculative opportunity, but many of New York's more modest merchants also fit in the category. Almost half the group identified themselves as merchants, a designation which implies full-time involvement at least in shopkeeping if not in importing and exporting.

Daniel Honan and William Sharpas, both of whom claimed the title gentleman, exemplify the wealthy residents who were able to attain modest commercial standing through a single transaction. Honan, who served as deputy secretary of the province, placed in the fifth interval of the scale by bringing from London in May 1702 three trunks, two cases, and one box of sundry goods worth £298.13.6. Sharpas, the perennial clerk of New York City, placed in the same bracket by importing from Barbados in October 1701 a bale, a box, and 276 ells of white ozenbrigs, or osnaburgs.[8]

Elizabeth Jourdain, whose business activities illustrate the increased economic and legal role which colonial conditions af-

[7] Name of master, number of times he imported in his own vessel/total number of times he imported: Derrick Adolph, 2/2; Peter Adolph, 2/2; Peter Bayard, 0/2; Benjamin Bill, 0/1; John Bond, 0/1; Samuel Bourdet, 2/2; John Corbett, 0/4; Claese Evertse, 0/2; John Finch, 0/1; Andrew Grevenraedt, 1/3; Lucas Kierstead, 1/1; Andrew Law, 1/1; Benjamin Norwood, 0/1; Symon Pasco, 0/1; William Peartree, 1/2; Abraham Sandford, 2/3; Giles Shelly, 0/4; Robert Sincklair, 1/1; Charles Sleigh, 1/1; Lancaster Symes, 0/3; Gabriel Thiboux, 0/1; Nicholas Thinehoven, 1/1.

[8] "Lords of Trade to Lord Cornbury," Dec. 18, 1701, *DRNY*, IV, 925–26; *HMR*, pp. 35, 54.

forded women, and Saul Brown, a Jewish merchant, are probably more representative of the middle-ranking importers and exporters. Mrs. Jourdain carried on the business of her deceased mariner husband, Henry, who in 1701 imported English goods valued at £61.16.0. Her importation in 1702 of £140.13.1 worth of merchandise, including 173 ells of white ozenbrigs, placed the Jourdains in the fifth interval. The large quantity of cloth which Elizabeth Jourdain brought to New York suggests that she, like Saul Brown, who ranked in the seventh bracket, operated a dry goods store. Brown's widow Esther also carried on his business, and at her death in 1708 had an inventory which included many yards of varied cloths, as well as a large supply of alcoholic spirits.[9]

Importers and exporters in the eighth, ninth, and tenth intervals, which includes 31 English and French residents and only 14 Dutch, made up the elite of New York's mercantile community. These leaders recognized the central position of commerce in their lives by regularly describing themselves as merchants, and even some of those who used other designations could have claimed the title.[10] In the highest bracket, Brandt Schuyler and William Smith, identified as gentlemen because they held the important offices of alderman and councilor respectively, began their careers as merchants and continued upon occasion to call themselves such. Another gentleman, Roger Brett, a vestryman of Trinity Church who ranked in the eighth interval, was the husband of Katherine Rombouts, the daughter of François Rombouts, a wealthy merchant. Rombouts's third wife Helena, classified as a widow in 1702, ranked in the ninth bracket and may

[9] *HMR;* inventory of the estate of Esther Brown, July 1708, Klapper Library, Queens College, City University of New York.

[10] The percentage of importers and exporters in each interval of the scale of commercial importance who described themselves as merchants: 1st and 2nd, 16 percent; 3rd and 4th, 24 percent; 5th, 42 percent; 6th, 50 percent; 7th, 53 percent; 8th, 71 percent; 9th, 87 percent; 10th, 84 percent.

have been the outstanding businesswoman of the community. In July 1702 she imported 2,647 gallons of rum from the West Indies and exported to London hundreds of pelts, including 419 deerskins and 270 raccoon furs.[11]

Like their counterparts in other colonies, the merchants ranking in the top brackets were active in a variety of fields of trade.

Table 5. Leading merchants according to the scale of commercial importance

Name	Goods	Rum	Wine	Exports	Total
Rip Van Dam	10	10	10	10	40
Abraham De Peyster	10	10	10	6	36
Gabriel Minvielle	9	9	8	8	34
Richard Willett	9	9	10	2	30
Stephen De Lancey	10	10	0	9	29
Cornelius De Peyster	7	10	6	6	29
Thomas Noell	10	10	2	6	28
Benjamin Aske	10	7	0	10	27
Matthew Ling	10	9	8	0	27
Ouzeel Van Sweeten	10	7	0	10	27
Benjamin Faneuil	8	10	0	8	26
John Norbury	10	10	0	6	26
Ebenezer Willson	4	7	6	9	26
Isaac R. Marques	9	8	0	8	25
William Smith	10	7	8	0	25
John Burrows	10	7	0	7	24
Brandt Schuyler	8	7	0	9	24
Walter Thong	7	9	0	8	24
John Chollwell	9	9	6	0	24

Source: *HMR*

All 19 of the men in the highest interval of the overall scale participated in at least three of the four categories of commerce— the importation of goods, of rum, and of wine, and the exportation of furs (Table 5). In the ninth bracket 12 of the 17 shippers took part in at least three endeavors, and in the eighth, 13 of the 14 were involved in two, and the other person in three.

Seven of the top 19 merchants engaged in all four enterprises. Rip Van Dam gained the maximum score of 40 with 10 points

[11] Con. Lib., May 9, 1696, XXIII, 234–36; Mar. 13, 1703, XXV, 208–9; Min. Ves., pp. 55, 57, 62; *Coll. NYGBS,* IX, 54; *HMR,* pp. 57–58, 68.

in each specialty. Abraham De Peyster, who was the second foremost merchant, achieved 6 points for exportation and 10 points in each of the three other fields.

Merchants in the middle and the lower ranks tended to participate in fewer areas of trade. Four of the merchants in the seventh bracket, 7 in the sixth, and 15 in the fifth engaged in only one type of trade. In the four lowest brackets combined, only 5 individuals were active in more than one area.

No means exists to measure exactly how great a share of the combined import-export business the city's outstanding merchants controlled, but separate examinations show that the persons in the top brackets accounted for much of the volume in each of the four categories of trade. In light of this fact, the large representation of English and French residents among their numbers is all the more important.

Importers included in this survey brought £57,116.11.6 worth of general merchandise into the province during the years 1701 and 1702. The merchants in the tenth or highest interval of the scale accounted for £32,711.8.9 or 57 percent of the total. Stephen De Lancey, a Frenchman, alone imported £3,667.12.4 or 6 percent of the final amount.[12] The 16 shippers in the ninth bracket brought in an additional £11,573.6.6 or 20 percent of the whole, and those in the eighth, 10 percent. In other words, merchants in the top three intervals accounted for 87 percent of the total.

A few merchants dominated the importation of rum. The top 10 percent of the rum importers accounted for £674.3.9 or 46 percent of the total duties of £1,459.6.1, and the most active 20 percent paid for 68 percent of the customs. Importation of wine was even more consolidated. The three leading merchants of the 35 engaged in the trade controlled 64 percent of the business, and the next most prominent three another 11 percent. The three

[12] *HMR*.

leaders, Abraham De Peyster, Rip Van Dam, and Richard Willett, respectively accounted for £350, £182, and £108 of the entire 1701–1702 taxation of £1,004.14.2.[13]

Exporting was the least centralized of the shipping endeavors. The six men in the top interval paid £148.11.3 in duties, or 34 percent of the total of £441.19.6. Ouzeel Van Sweeten, who paid £44.3.6 on his cargoes, was by far the leading exporter.[14] Men in the ninth interval accounted for 21 percent of the total sum, those in the eighth range 15 percent, and those in the seventh, 11 percent.

Manhattan's merchant princes dealt in an astonishing variety of wares. In 1698, 1699, and 1700 a scion of one of New York's great Dutch families, Jacobus Van Cortlandt, who ranked in the eighth interval of the 1701–1702 scale, did business with Boston, the West Indies, London, and Amsterdam. He sold cotton, indigo, lime juice, molasses, salt and sugar which West Indian merchants sent him. Despite his objections that slave ships from Madagascar and Guinea had brought a glut of blacks to the port, he disposed of West Indian slaves on several occasions. Van Cortlandt complained that he could not dispose of cherry brandy on the public house row because New York's tipplers preferred rum, but he finally managed to sell a consignment of it. In June 1698 he sent 32 half-barrels of flour worth £52.12.8½ to Captain Thomas Clarke, one of his many West Indian associates, and a month later Van Cortlandt mailed his Boston correspondent William Welsteed £109.12.0 for large women's gloves, yellow flannel, crepe, blankets, and other items for the New York market. Van Cortlandt sought logwood for the European market and wines for Amsterdam, sent cocoa and sugar to England, and requested his regular London contact John Blackall to supply him with thousands of pins, black flow-

---

[13] *Ibid.*   [14] *Ibid.*

ered satins, and cloth which he warned had to be of a fashionable color if it were to sell in the New York market.[15]

Wealthy merchants added to their riches by purchasing merchant vessels. Frederick Philipse, a councilor whose estate lay outside New York but who was active in the city's commerce, owned the *New York Merchant,* one of the three-masted ships which were the mainstay of the transatlantic route. He also owned the *Frederick* and the *New York,* sloops of the type which dominated the West Indian and the mainland intercolonial trade. The latter, obtained in 1694 from the New York shipbuilder Elias Puddington, had a burden of 50 tons, near the maximum for this class of single-masted vessel which carried a yard or two of topsail as well as a fore-and-aft mainsail. Caleb Heathcote, another councilor who participated in Manhattan's mercantile life while residing outside the city, paid the New York shipbuilder Jean Machet £315 in 1693 for the *Loyall Merchant,* a brigantine of 80 to 90 tons burden.[16] Two-masted vessels at least partially square-rigged, brigs and brigantines usually plied the waters between New York and the West Indies.

Rip Van Dam, Manhattan's leading shipper, owned the bark *John and Michael.* Abraham De Peyster, who ranked second among the city's merchants, spent £315 in 1698 to buy the *Hester,* a vessel seized by the government for alleged illegal trade.

---

[15] Van Cortlandt to: Mr. Roe, Apr. 16, 1698; Alexander Hamelton, May 24, 1698; Miles Mayhew, Apr. 15 and June 23, 1698; Barnabas Jenkins, June 30, 1698; John Smith, June 8 and Aug. 18, 1698; Thomas Whitson, Sept. 15, 1698; Clarck [Clarke], June 6, 1698; Welsteed, Apr. 4 and July 11, 1698; Richard Miles, Apr. 22, 1700; William Peartree, Mar. 10, 1698; Blackall, May 2, 1698, and Apr. 28, 1700.

[16] Elizabeth Donnan, ed., *Documents Illustrative of the History of the Slave Trade to America* (Washington, D.C., 1932), III, 442; Puddington to Philipse, bill of sale, June 13, 1694; Machet to Heathcote, bill of sale, July 27, 1693, Con. Lib., XVIII, 334–36; XXI, 199–200.

The Jewish merchant Isaac Rodriques Marques, who ranked in the highest interval on the scale, owned the ship *Dolphin,* and his co-religionist Joseph Bueno, whose enterprises placed him in the eighth bracket, owned "sundry vessels." [17]

In addition, some top New York merchants held shares in vessels. Abraham De Peyster, the owner of the *Hester,* held one-fourth of the 295-ton ship *William and Mary.* William Morris, who ranked in the ninth bracket, owned one-fourth of the 90-ton *Blossom.* At his death in 1706, Robert Allison, who ranked in the eight interval in 1701–1702, held half of the ship *John and Michael* and two-thirds of the sloop *Rubey.* [18]

Enterprising merchants also underwrote the privateering expeditions which began in New York in the 1690s. Respectable citizens found tempting the legal booty made available by the war with France and by the struggles against pirates. William Livingston, an immigrant from Scotland who quickly gained wealth and political influence, helped raise £6000 to outfit Captain William Kidd's ill-fated mission to rid the Madagascar coast of the Jolly Roger. Although he eventually suffered execution for piracy, Kidd himself was a man of standing in New York and the third husband of Sarah Oort, a well-born widow first of a rich merchant and then of a sea captain. Jacob Blydenburgh, an established Manhattan trader, assured himself of part of the treasure returned to New York by making loans valued at

[17] Van Dam v. William Pead, Sept. 10, 1701; Barent Rynders v. Lewis Gomez, Abraham de Lucena, and Rachell Bueno, executors of Joseph Bueno, Nov. 30, 1708; George Norton v. Rodriques Marques, July 23, 1704, New York City, Minutes of the Mayor's Court, Hall of Records, New York; Rodriques Marques and Henry Jourdain, business agreement, June 27, 1700, Con. Lib., XXVIII, 187–88; Charles McLean Andrews, *The Colonial Period of American History* (New Haven, 1937), III, 180n–181n.

[18] De Peyster to Valentine Cruger, bill of sale, Aug. 1, 1696; Morris and James Mills, business agreement, Nov. 11, 1697, Con. Lib., XXI, 182–83; XXI, 256–58; inventory of the estate of Allison, 1706, Klapper Library.

£1500 to several of the seamen in Kidd's crew. Blydenburgh promised to supply the mariners with shirts, waistcoats, shoes, stockings, rum, sugar, tobacco, thread, buttons, spoons, hats, and other items in return for one-third of the money, plate, bullion, gold, Negroes, and other gains of the voyage.[19]

Pace-setters in every aspect of commerce, New York's foremost merchants occasionally put their talents to dubious uses. Participants in illegal trade required resources at least as great as those of honest shippers, and indeed Governor Bellomont complained that piracy and smuggling were "the beloved twins of the Merchants of this place." In 1698 the collector and the searcher of the customs found a quantity of illicit goods in the house of Ouzeel Van Sweeten, who ranked in the highest interval on the scale of commercial importance. Van Sweeten, aided by his fellow merchants, seized the officers and held them captive until the governor sent troops to rescue them.[20]

European vessels visited New York most frequently in the blustery months between November and April. London had become the key point of contact in the city's transatlantic trade. Occasionally bottoms destined for Manhattan would stop at Amsterdam on their voyage, but of the 21 which dropped anchor in the harbor during 1701 and 1702, 18 identified London and 3 Bristol as their terminal ports.

Sloops and brigs from the West Indies, the Atlantic Islands of the Azores and Madeira, and South America appeared in the city mostly in the spring months of April, May, June, and in August. The English colonies of Jamaica and Barbados, which

[19] Herbert Levi Osgood, *The American Colonies in the Eighteenth Century* (New York, 1924), I, 532–33; Frank Monaghan, "William Kidd," *Dictionary of American Biography* (New York, 1933), X, 368; Joseph Blydenburgh and various sailors on the *Adventure Galley*, Aug. 6–26, 1696, business agreements, Con. Lib., XXI, 131–42.

[20] "Earl of Bellomont to the Lord of Trade," May 18, June 22, and Dec. 15, 1698, *DRNY*, IV, 303, 324.

respectively accounted for 24 and 19 of the 78 entries, dominated the trade. Antigua (9), Nevis (7), Madeira (4), St. Chris-
topher (3), Surinam (3), Bermuda (2), Easter Cape or Easy
Cape (2), Fayal (2), Isquebad or Isaquiba (2), Saltitudos or Sal-
titudas (1), and Santo Domingo (1) provided the remainder.

Ships from the other mainland English colonies crowded New
York in August but also maintained contact during the other
months. Boston was the most frequent trading partner. Massachusetts sloops, with 26 calls in 1701 and 1702, made more
than twice as many entries as the bottoms from Carolina (3),
Connecticut (3), Philadelphia (2), Rhode Island (2), New Castle
(1), and Virginia (1) combined (Table 6).

The change in New York's trade patterns put the city's Dutch
merchants, who had made their business connections in Amsterdam and her colonies, at a serious disadvantage. Although the
Articles of Capitulation allowed Dutch New Yorkers, once they
applied to the governor for a certificate of freedom and residence, to carry on trade with England or her American colonies,
most of the Dutch lacked the family and ethnic group ties which
would have provided them with agency relationships and
sources of credit in London and the English provinces. Without
these ties, they had little prospect of success in the commerce of
the seventeenth and eighteenth centuries.[21]

In contrast, English merchants in New York frequently used
relatives in England and the West Indies to sustain their business. Caleb Heathcote, the councilor, may have traded with his
London merchant brother, Sir Gilbert. Matthew Ling, who
ranked in the tenth interval of the scale of commercial activity,
frequently did business in Nevis, the home of William Ling, his
only brother. William Smith, who also ranked in the top
bracket, established his son William as a merchant in the West

---

[21] "Articles of Capitulation," p. 251.

Table 6. Ships docking in the port of New York in 1701 and 1702

Months	Europe			West Indies, Atlantic Islands, and South America			Mainland colonies			Total		
	1701	1702	1701–2	1701	1702	1701–2	1701	1702	1701–2	1701	1702	1701–2
January	1	1	2	0	0	0	0	1	1	1	2	3
February	2	0	2	0	0	0	0	2	2	2	2	4
March	3	1	4	5	3	8	1	1	2	9	5	14
April	0	3	3	8	7	15	2	2	4	10	12	22
May	0	1	1	9	2	11	1	1	2	10	4	14
June	1	0	1	4	7	11	4	3	7	9	10	19
July	1	0	1	3	2	5	2	0	2	6	2	8
August	0	0	0	8	4	12	6	5	11	14	9	23
September	0	1	1	4	2	6	0	0	0	4	3	7
October	0	1	1	5	2	7	3	0	3	8	3	11
November	1	2	3	0	2	2	1	4	5	2	8	10
December	2	0	2	2	0	2	1	0	1	5	0	5

Source: *HMR*

Indies. Captain Thomas Clarke of Jamaica received goods from his New York–based father. William Peartree, mayor of New York from 1703 to 1706, maintained contact with his brother in Jamaica. When William moved to the island, he initiated a business correspondence with his son-in-law back in New York.[22]

Huguenot merchants in New York, through the French exile community in London, duplicated the ethnic contacts of their English competitors. The dealings of the Huguenot Matthew Collineau illustrate the operation of the intra-ethnic group connection. Early in 1696, Collineau left London with the power of attorney from the widow of Elias Nezereau to collect debts due her from their fellow Huguenot John Vincent of New York. In America, Collineau agreed to send to Jeremiah Tothill, an Anglo-American merchant, a shipment of goods upon his return to England. Collineau never fulfilled the bargain, and the courts ordered his fellow Huguenot merchants, Elias Boudinot, Sr., and Elias Boudinot, Jr., whom he left in charge of his affairs, to compensate Tothill.[23]

Jewish merchants likewise maintained connections with their co-religionists living in English territory. Isaac Rodriques Marques, who ranked in the highest commercial bracket, in 1700 sold the bark *Dolphin* for £600 to three Jews, two of whom lived in London. His brother Jacob Rodriques Marques of New York bought a quarter share as did Joseph Henriques of London, and Abraham Menders of London took the other half share. Jews such as Aaron Lamogo of Jamaica, Solomon Levy

[22] Gilbert Heathcote to Stephen De Lancey and Ebenezer Willson, power of attorney, Jan. 22, 1705; William Ling to Caleb Cooper, power of attorney, Feb. 13, 1705, Con. Lib., XXVI, 51–52; XXV, 368–69; *HMR;* Van Cortlandt Letter Book.

[23] Magdalen Nezereau to Matthew Collineau, power of attorney, Dec. 13, 1695, Con. Lib., XXI, 151–53; Jeremiah Tothill v. Matthew Collineau, foreign attachment, July 8, 1701, New York City, Minutes of the Mayor's Court.

Maduro of Curaçao; and a Gomez of London frequently appear as creditors and debtors in the inventory of estate taken after Isaac Marques's death in 1708.[24]

Both Huguenots and Jews also made use of relatives based where they could help them compete effectively in New York commerce. Thomas Bayeux, a Huguenot who did business with England, acted as attorney for his brother, John Bayeux, a London merchant, and the Jewish merchant Jacob Nunes served in the same capacity for his London-based brother, Abraham. The family of the Huguenot immigrant Augustus Jay for many years maintained commercial correspondence and connections with the family of his brother-in-law, Stephen Peloquin of Bristol, England. The Huguenot Benjamin Faneuil shipped regularly to and from Boston, the home port of his brother Peter.[25]

Dutch New Yorkers with roots in the elite families of New Amsterdam could sometimes match the advantages of the English and Huguenots. These Dutch merchant princes had accommodated themselves to the new regime, and had developed personal and political ties with the conquering nation. Rip Van Dam, the only shipper to score ten points in all four areas of commercial endeavor, was chosen by the London merchant Michael Kinkaid as his attorney in New York. In addition, Van Dam's son-in-law was the Englishman Walter Thong who divided his time between Manhattan and London. Abraham De Peyster stood second on the scale of mercantile importance and

[24] Isaac Rodriques Marques to Abraham Menders, Joseph Henriques, and Jacob Rodriques Marques, bill of sale, Dec. 10, 1700, Con. Lib., XXIII, 291–92; inventory of the estate of Isaac Rodriques Marques, 1708, Klapper Library.

[25] John Bayeux to Thomas Bayeux, power of attorney, Nov. 28, 1706; Abraham Nunes to Joseph Nunes, power of attorney, Jan. 18, 1700, Con. Lib., XXVI, 260–61; XXIII, 302; Jay Paper Collection, Butler Library, Columbia University; *HMR;* Mrs. John A. Weisse, *A History of the Bethune Family Together with a Sketch of the Faneuil Family* (New York, 1884).

was a close political ally of Governor Bellomont. Ouzeel Van Sweeten, who ranked in the top commercial bracket, spent enough time in England to be described as a Londoner when he embarked for New York in 1692.[26]

The activities of Jacobus Van Cortlandt, who ranked in the eight interval on the 1701–702 scale, illustrate how a well-connected Dutch merchant could prosper. He was born in 1658 and as the son of Oloff Stevensen Van Cortlandt automatically became part of New York's elite. He further established himself in 1691 by his marriage to Eva, the stepdaughter of the extraordinarily wealthy Frederick Philipse.[27]

As a member of an established family, Van Cortlandt could depend on the support of other members of the Dutch mercantile elite. In February 1701 he sent to London aboard the ship *Leventhorp* two casks of cocoa consigned to the stepbrother of his wife, Adolph Philipse, who was in the English capital. How Van Cortlandt established his connection with John Blackall, the London merchant with whom he corresponded regularly is not known, but friendship with his fellow Dutch New Yorker Rip Van Dam provided the recommendation which enabled him in May 1700 to add Thomas Bond of London to his list of contacts. Association with Ouzeel Van Sweeten brought Van Cortlandt in touch with another London businessman, Robert Hackshaw.[28]

---

[26] Michael Kinkaid to Rip Van Dam, power of attorney, Nov. 23, 1703; John Blankly to Walter Thong, power of attorney, Mar. 17, 1702; Valentine Cruger to Ouzeel Van Sweeten, power of attorney, Apr. 16, 1692, Con. Lib., XXV, 204–5, 170–74; XVIII, 227–29; John Ross Delafield, "Walter Thong of New York and His Forefathers," *NYGB Rec.*, LXXXIII (Oct. 1952), 204.

[27] L. Effingham De Forest, *The Van Cortlandt Family* (New York, 1930), p. 4; Howard S. F. Randolph, "The Hardenbrook Family," *NYGB Rec.*, LXX (Apr. 1939), 129.

[28] Bills of lading, Feb. 20 and July 3, 1701, in "Jacobus Van Cortlandt's Shipments from the Port of New York, 1695–1702," *New-York Historical So-*

Van Cortlandt could move as an equal among these English merchants. His contacts with Dutch merchants in Curaçao, including the widows Sara Abendano and Neeltien Visschers, made him a valuable associate for English merchants anxious to expand their business spheres. He could inform his London associate John Blackall of shipments headed for Amsterdam, and he could consign goods belonging to the Holland merchant William De Grandt to the London trader Edward Browne.[29]

Van Cortlandt's success, then, was mostly the result of his extensive business with Englishmen. More than 90 percent of the approximately 110 Van Cortlandt letters which have survived from the 1698 to 1700 period were directed to English rather than Dutch correspondents. A number of these English contacts were friends from New York or their relatives. Van Cortlandt had extensive dealings with William Peartree, who was in Jamaica at the time, including advice on the former mayor's business matters and legal problems back in Manhattan. In the West Indies, Van Cortlandt traded with John Smith, one son of the New York merchant, William Smith. Captain Thomas Clarke, another son of a New Yorker, gave Van Cortlandt power of attorney as his "trusty and loving friend.[30]

For Jacobus Van Cortlandt there was little disadvantage in being Dutch. His wife could send greetings and a firkin of butter to William Peartree's spouse, and the former mayor would send the best Jamaica planks to New York to make a chest for his friend's lady. In his first letter to the London merchant Thomas

---

ciety Quarterly Bulletin, XX (Oct. 1936), 118, 120; Van Cortlandt to Bond, May 16, 1700, Van Cortlandt Letter Book.

[29] Bills of lading, June 9, 1701, Apr. 2 and June 20, 1702, "Van Cortlandt's Shipments," pp. 119, 121; Van Cortlandt to Blackall, July 18, 1698, Van Cortlandt Letter Book.

[30] Van Cortlandt to Peartree and to William Smith, several entries, Van Cortlandt Letter Book; Clarke to Van Cortlandt, power of attorney, May 22, 1696, Con. Lib., XXI, 118.

Bond, Van Cortlandt could ask him to remind his brother John Bond, the captain of the ship *Endeavour,* to obtain one "Eyvory foote rule with foure points and my name on it." Most important Van Cortlandt could inform John Blackall that he had a one-third interest in the 90 to 100 ton *Hopewell* which Nicholas Gerritson was loading for the Isle of Wight and Amsterdam, and ask his London partner to provide him with £300 sterling on the brig. Van Cortlandt might add "Pray fail not in so doing," but he could be assured of cooperation.[31]

Most Dutch New Yorkers were not so fortunate as Jacobus Van Cortlandt. Even less were they able to match the ability of either established or younger, well-connected Englishmen to immigrate to Manhattan and quickly gain commercial prominence. Caleb Cooper, described in 1703 as "formerly of London," arrived in New York at least in time to import "one case with one looking glass" from England in March 1701 on the *Antigua Merchant.* During the two years surveyed, Cooper, who ranked in the eighth interval, was able to place himself among the city's leading merchants through his dealings with Massachusetts, the West Indies, the Canary Islands, and Europe.[32]

The rise to prominence of the English and French merchants exemplifies the way in which New York became an English city during the last quarter of the seventeenth century. The government did not pursue a policy of eliminating the city's Dutch from positions of wealth and influence. Indeed, a goodly number of burghers who had been affluent and important in the days of New Amsterdam received many favors from the English. But the conquest made change inevitable, and the out-

---

[31] Van Cortlandt to Peartree, Mar. 10 and June 6, 1698, and May 28, 1700; to Thomas Bond, May 16, 1700; to Blackall, July 18, 1698, Van Cortlandt Letter Book.

[32] Michael Kinkaid to Rip Van Dam, power of attorney, Nov. 23, 1703, Con. Lib., XXV, 204–5; *HMR.*

come left ordinary Dutch residents of Manhattan unable to compete effectively. For many of the Dutch, the change limited the horizons which their fathers had come to the New World to expand, and even the streets of a growing New York gave evidence of their lower status.

4 ❧ Social Geography

New York's population grew rapidly after the English conquest, and the city expanded to keep pace. In the 1670s citizens
were already moving north of the palisaded breastworks of Wall
Street, where the gates were closed between nine at night and
daybreak. By the end of the century, Manhattan's population
filled the Smith's Valley along the East River and reached
Maiden Lane. The defenses at Wall Street had crumbled, and in
1699 materials salvaged from the rubble were put to another use
in the construction of the new city hall.[1]

The growing city reflected in geography the social and economic changes which occurred within the population in the
wake of the English take-over. New York in the 1670s remained
a Dutch city, and according to a promotional tract of the time,
their characteristic buildings, two story brick and stone struc-
tures topped by lovely red and black tile roofs, dominated the
harbor and provided a most "pleasing Aspect" to passengers on
ships approaching the docks.[2] Dutch architecture retained its influence in New York, but by the end of the century the English
lived in the city's finest houses and the descendents of the

[1] *Min. Com. Coun.*, Jan. 11, 1676, I, 8; Oswald Garrison Villard, "The
Early History of Wall Street, 1653–1789," in Maud Wilder Goodwin *et al.*,
eds., *Half-Moon Series: Papers on Historic New York* (New York, 1898), I,
112–13.

[2] Daniel Denton, *A Brief Description of New York, Formerly Called New
Netherland* (London, 1670; reprinted Cleveland, 1902), p. 2.

founders often made their homes in the less desirable areas of the island.

Dutch residents composed 81 percent of the population in 1677, and their accents were heard proportionately on almost every street of the city. They accounted for 83 percent of the ethnically identifiable families on the most fashionable streets, which were usually located near the fort at the southwest corner of Manhattan Island. That section of the Water Side where the north side of Pearl Street is presently located was the home of some of New York's wealthiest citizens, including the Dutch merchant John Hendricks De Bruyn. The Dutch also contributed 83 percent of the inhabitants of the streets of middle standing, which included parts of the major thoroughfares leading north from the dock area at the southeast tip of the island. Broad Street, formerly composed of Heere and Prince Grachts (canals filled in 1676), was typical of streets in this median range. Finally, 75 percent of the residents who had their dwellings on the poorer streets, which included several of the east-west roads at the center of the city, bore Dutch names. Smith Street Lane, which today is Beaver Street between William and Broad Streets, fits into this category (Map 1 and Table 7).[3]

Signs of growth appear throughout the records of New York in the late seventeenth century. The mayors and the members of the Common Council worked constantly to enhance the salubrity and attractiveness of the city by improving public services. More important, the authorities controlled the public lands and used the sale of them to ensure the orderliness of the city's expansion.

[3] *Min. Com. Coun.*, July 24, 1677, I, 50–63; David T. Valentine, *History of the City of New York* (New York, 1853), pp. 319–30. Since there are no good maps of this period, I have compiled Maps 1 and 2 from a variety of sources. They are only intended as sketch maps.

Table 7. New York City's major streets, 1677: wealth and ethnic composition

Street	Average tax (shillings)	Dutch	English/ French	Other/ Unknown
Smith St. Lane	5.3	6	2	1
Smith St.	5.7	21	3	1
Broadway, north of Wall	6.0	3	1	0
Mill St.	6.2	5	0	0
Marketfield St.	6.4	8	1	1
Wall St.	6.6	9	4	2
Broadway, south of Wall, east side	7.0	15	6	1
Beaver St.	7.6	24	4	1
High St., south side	7.96	12	0	1
The Smith's Valley	7.98	19	2	2
Broad St., east side	8.3	10	7	1
Broad St., west side	8.71	18	1	0
Pearl St.	8.78	17	1	0
Water Side, from Broad St. to Burger's Path	10.0	9	4	0
Broadway, south of Wall, west side	10.2	9	7	0
Water Side, from Burger's Path to the Smith's Valley	12.0	9	2	0
High St., north side	13.8	13	1	0
Water Side, from Market- field to Broad St.	14.1	8	3	1
Marketfield and Broadway	16.2	9	0	0
Stone St.	18.0	6	2	0
Water Side, from Market- field south	24.0	1	1	0

Sources: *Min. Com. Coun.,* 1, 50–62; Valentine, *History of New York,* pp. 319–30; and others mentioned previously

As early as 1675 the government provided for the weekly collection of refuse. According to the Common Council's directive, New York's householders were to sweep the dirt and filth into neat piles each Saturday, and the cartmen of the city were to remove this garbage to the waterside. Uncooperative citizens were subject to a three shilling fine and negligent carters to loss of their position. At the same time, the Council renewed its efforts to prohibit the free roaming of cows, horses, and pigs through Manhattan's streets. A few months later the city fathers

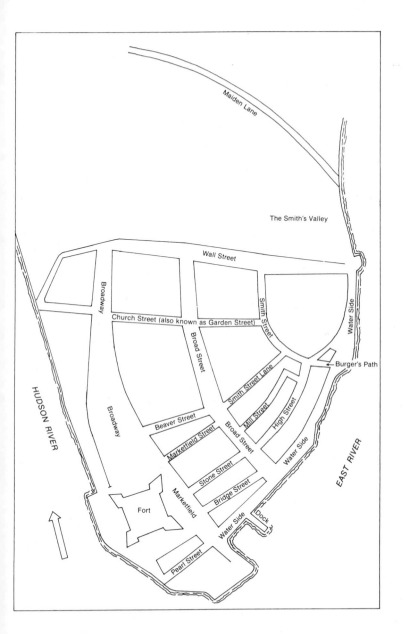

Map 1. New York City around 1677

ordered both slaughterhouses and tanneries removed to the out-
skirts of the town.[4]

Paving of New York roads began in 1657 and continued
throughout the last quarter of the century. Each householder was
responsible for paving, at his own expense, a specified distance
from his own doorfront toward the center of the street. Covered
with good pebblestones, the new roads were graded to allow
drainage into the waters surrounding the island. These pathways
needed constant attention and periodic relaying; Beaver Street,
for example, was paved four times between 1684 and 1701. The
waterfront area posed special problems, and persons who lived
on streets along the shore had to build wharves 30 feet broad between their property and the low water mark.[5]

The people of Manhattan drew their water from wells dug in
the their streets. At various times during the latter part of the
seventeenth century the Common Council designated well sites
throughout the city and paid half of the expense of their construction. The inhabitants of the neighborhoods thus supplied
with water paid the remaining costs, and a local resident was
made responsible for maintenance of each of the stone wells.[6]

Clean, paved streets and available water assisted the authorities in their efforts to prevent and fight fires, the most grave
threat to the growing city. The lawmakers prohibited the storage
of hay or straw in or near dwellings, forbade the dumping of
smoldering ashes into the streets, and appointed masons like
Tobias Stoutenburgh, Olphert Suerts, and Dirck Vanderburgh to
insure that the inhabitants kept their chimneys in good working

---

[4] *Min. Com. Coun.*, Nov. 24, 1675, June 7, 1676, I, 13, 20–21.

[5] *Ibid.*, May 24, 1684, Feb. 11, 1693, Mar. 26, 1696, May 24, 1701, I,
151, 314–15, 402; II, 114. On the erection of wharves, *ibid.*, June 16, 1696,
I, 406.

[6] *Ibid.*, Sept. 10, 1686, I, 181; Oct. 4, 1698, II, 57.

order. For the tragic times when fires did start, the city required its householders to have water buckets available.[7]

Along with cleaning and protecting the city, New Yorkers in the 1680s and 1690s made other, more vigorous efforts to improve its appearance, while simultaneously adding money to the municipal coffers. This was accomplished by selling highly desirable public lands along the waterfront to make possible the construction of fashionable new streets there. In 1686, in order to raise money to pay for the charter received from Governor Thomas Dongan, the Common Council created Dock Street. They divided the area between the weighhouse and the City Hall into lots, most of which measured 80 feet by 24 feet. Five years later, as a means of financing a new ferryhouse and a new markethouse, the lawmakers partitioned the land between Burger's Path and the blockhouse at Wall Street into lots, most of which were 42 feet broad. The authorities continued the operation in the following year by laying out the remaining East River region from Wall Street north to the holdings of Alderman William Beeckman, and in 1694 they designated the entire stretch of highway between Burger's Path and Beeckman's lands as Queen Street (Map 2).[8]

Rapidly becoming the dominant commercial group in New York, Englishmen also rushed to gain social prominence by obtaining sites on the new blocks. Governor Thomas Dongan, the gentleman John West, and the merchant William Cox were among those who bought Dock Street lots. In 1691 the municipality guaranteed that Queen Street would become one of the

[7] *Ibid.,* Nov. 13, 1676, Oct. 8, 1679, Feb. 28, 1687, I, 23–29, 73, 187; Arthur Everett Peterson, *New York as an Eighteenth Century Municipality: Prior to 1731* (New York, 1917), pp. 177–81.

[8] *Min. Com. Coun.,* Oct. 13, 1687, Feb. 14, 1688, Mar. 24, 1688, Dec. 5, 1691, Aug. 9, 1692, Oct. 13, 1694, I, 190, 193–95, 259, 278–79, 370.

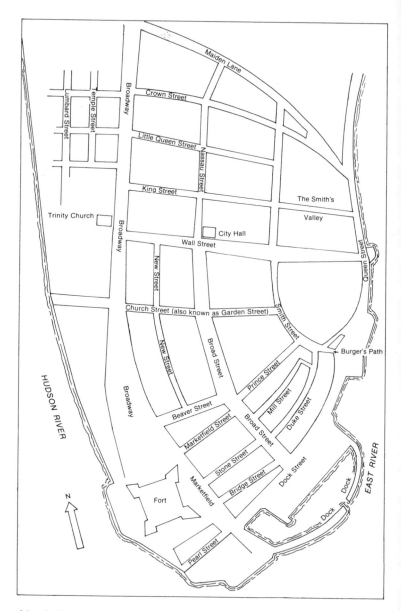

Map 2. New York City around 1703

city's most attractive thoroughfares by requiring that all houses built along it be 25 feet broad, two stories tall, and of brick or stone construction at least at the gable end. Englishmen, along with Manhattan's most affluent Dutch, flocked to purchase property in the area. The merchants Thomas Clarke, Miles Forster, George Heathcote, William Merritt, William Morris, John Theobald, and Ebenezer Willson were among the English residents who joined Frederick Philipse, Jacobus Van Cortlandt, Stephen Van Cortlandt, and other Dutch inhabitants as owners there.[9]

English New Yorkers also demonstrated their newly gained influence by purchasing large plots of land on the northern edges of the city for development. Late in 1699, for a "valuable consideration," the mayor, aldermen, and Common Council conveyed to John Hutchins, Gentleman, who served as an alderman and as a vestryman of Trinity Church; William Huddleston, Gentleman, an attorney who immigrated from England in 1695; and John Rodman, Gentleman, who was a physician and merchant, a sizable parcel of Hudson waterfront, which they promised to improve by laying a wharf and leveling the river bank. The property, which ran 277 feet 6 inches on its broadest side, represented a large increment to the western boundary of their already extensive holdings in the area. In 1701, Philip French, an eminent merchant and politician, paid the municipality £195 for eight East River lots, which measured a total of 208 feet at the river, 125 feet along the sides, and 216 feet on the street.[10]

---

[9] New York City, Water Grants, 1686–1907, Dept. of Real Estate, New York, Liber A, especially pp. 12–13, 29–30, 40–41, 76–78; *Min. Com. Coun.*, Dec. 5, 1691, I, 259–60.

[10] *Min. Com. Coun.*, Sept. 29, 1697, II, 14; Min. Ves., p. 33; Paul M. Hamlin and Charles E. Baker, *Supreme Court of Judicature of the Province of New York, 1691–1704* (New York, 1959), III, 104–5; Charles Henry Jones, *Genealogy of the Rodman Family, 1620–1886* (Philadelphia, 1886), p. 14; New York City, Water Grants, Liber A, pp. 33–40.

Purchases of attractive residential lots and of speculative plots on the fringe of the growing city were just another symptom of the growing wealth and influence of the English and their Huguenot allies. By 1703 disproportionately large numbers of Englishmen and Huguenots made their residences on the wealthiest streets of the island. Dutch grandees lived side by side with the new elite, but the ordinary Dutch inhabitants who formed so large a part of the port's population filled the more modest streets and the poorer districts.[11]

The wealthiest streets were located at the southern tip of the island along the East River waterfront. The English and French outnumbered the Dutch 24 to 14 among the positively identified New Yorkers who lived in the Dock Ward section of Dock Street. The average resident of the district scored 7.98 and the typical homeowner 8.6 on the ten-interval scale used in this study to estimate relative financial standings. The English and the French held a 26 to 21 advantage in the section of the East Ward's Queen Street which was below Wall Street; the average inhabitant of this area scored only 5.2, but homeowners scored 8.66. Similarly, in the South Ward they outnumbered the Dutch 8 to 5 on Bridge Street, 5 to 4 on Dock Street, and 13 to 12 on Pearl Street, where the average residents scored 8.1, 7.4 and 6.9 respectively. Among New York's wealthiest blocks, only on Stone Street, where the Dutch outnumbered their English and French neighbors 11 to 3, did the descendants of the city's founders account for a sizable majority of the residents (Table 8).

Dock Street was the center of Dock Ward, the only area in the city in which the English and French formed a majority (52%) of the ethnically identified inhabitants. Dock Ward encompassed the area between Dock Street, Broad Street, Smith

[11] The Essay on Sources and Methods describes the materials used to locate the residences of New Yorkers both in 1677 and 1703.

Street, and Prince Street. On the ten-interval scale the residents of the Dock Ward scored higher (7.114) than those dwelling in any of the other four wards, the South (7.058), East (4.723), West (4.399), or North (4.087).

As a result, the Dock Ward section of Dock Street, where the English and French held a 24 to 14 majority, was the location of some of the most valuable property in the city, and was the

Table 8. New York City's major streets, 1703: wealth and ethnic composition

Street	Average score	Dutch	English/French
Church St.	2.6	4	0
Upper North Ward (Crown, King, Little Queen, Nassau Streets)	3.2	17	10
New St.	3.5	14	1
Queen St./Smith's Valley	4.2	41	29
Broadway, West Ward	4.7	38	26
Beaver St.	4.8	10	4
Wall St.	5.05	11	9
Smith St.	5.08	14	8
Broad St.	5.1	33	3
Queen St., south of Wall	5.2	21	26
Duke and Mill Streets	6.1	11	8
Pearl St.	6.7	12	13
Prince St.	6.8	12	5
Marketfield	7.0	4	2
Dock St., South Ward	7.4	4	5
Dock St., Dock Ward	7.98	14	24
Stone St.	8.0	11	3
Bridge St.	8.1	5	8
Burger's Path	9.75	2	2

Sources: 1703 assessment list and others mentioned previously

address of perhaps its most important residences. Jacobus Van Cortlandt, who became mayor in 1710, and between 1691 and 1710 served as alderman eight years and took part in eight of thirteen colonial assemblies, was its most noted Dutch resident. Van Cortlandt owned two houses assessed for a total of £450.[12]

[12] Howard S. F. Randolph, "The Hardenbrook Family," *NYGB Rec.,* LXX (Apr. 1939), 132; *Min. Com. Coun.,* Vols. I and II; New York Colony,

William Bradford, Philip French, and Robert Lurting were among Dock Street's leading English residents. Bradford, who had moved to New York from Philadelphia in 1693 and became the royal printer, had a house and estate worth £120. French, a merchant who served as mayor in 1702, had a house valued at £450. A native of Kelshall in Suffolk County, England, he had in 1694 married Anna Philipse, the daughter of Frederick Philipse, who was probably the wealthiest man in the colony. Lurting, a merchant whose assessment was £155, served as an alderman and an Anglican churchwarden in this period, and from 1726 to 1735 was the city's mayor.[13]

Stephen De Lancey was one of the foremost Huguenots on Dock Street. A native of Caen, he fled France after the revocation of the Edict of Nantes, sold his jewels in England, and made his way to New York. De Lancey, who quickly became a prominent merchant and served in the colonial legislature had an assessment of £275. Elias Boudinot, the son of a refugee Huguenot merchant of the same name, was another French resident of Dock Street. He paid taxes on £140, and his mother, who also had a house on the block, paid taxes on £130. Like many widows, who accounted for 24 of the 99 landlords included in this survey, Mrs. Boudinot opened her house to a tenant. In this case, the man in residence was Thomas Bayeux, a Huguenot merchant who in 1703 married her daughter, Magdeleine.[14]

Journal of the Votes and Proceedings of the General Assembly of the Colony of New York, 1691–1765 (New York, 1764–1766), Vol. I; New York City, Water Grants, Liber A, especially pp. 192–93.

[13] Samuel S. Purple, *Bradford Family: Genealogical Memorials of William Bradford, the Printer* (New York, 1873), p. 5; Edwin Ruthven Purple, "Varleth Family," *Contributions to the History of Ancient Families of New Amsterdam and New York* (New York, 1881), p. 92; *Min. Com. Coun.,* Sept. 29, 1702, II, 202; Sept. 29, 1726, Sept. 29, 1727, III, 394, 416; Con. Lib., Nov. 23, 1700, XXIII, 253–254; Min. Ves., p. 33.

[14] Valentine, *History of New York,* p. 231; *Coll. HSA,* pp. 5, 111.

Bayeux himself was fairly typical of many recently wed New Yorkers who did not establish separate households. At least 21 of the 61 tenants who married after 1695 lived with their immediate relatives.

Besides the lovely view and cooling breezes of an unspoiled bay, Dock Street's inhabitants were attracted to its proximity to the docks and customs facilities of the port. According to a ranking of Manhattan's streets in terms of the relative commercial importance of the importers and exporters in residence there, Dock Street, with a score of 95, was by far the most important in the city.[15] The section of Queen Street below Wall Street, where the English and French again held a majority, ranked second with 60 points, and the Queen Street/Smith's Valley area above Wall Street was third with 52. Broadway with 30 points and Pearl Street with 28 were a distant fourth and fifth.

Slaves were present in all areas of the city but were concentrated on streets inhabited by the wealthy. The fact that owners usually held only one or two bondsmen and the absence from the records of references to slave quarters indicate that the blacks lived in the households of their masters. On the ten-interval scale used to measure relative economic standing, nonslaveholders scored 4.3, slaveholders with from one to three blacks 6.9, and those with more than three, 8.5. The merchants, who were the wealthiest members of the community, held the largest bloc of bondsmen of any occupational group.[16] Inasmuch as the

---

[15] The Essay on Sources and Methods discusses this procedure.

[16] Occupational group, number of slaves, average number owned: merchants, 134, 2.1; widows, 83, 1.1; masters, 45, 1.1; bakers, 27, 1.3; gentlemen, 26, 1.7; victuallers, 21, 1.5; brewers, 20, 5.0; bolters, 18, 1.8; attorneys 16, 2.6; cordwainers, 15, 0.4; coopers, 13, 0.7; brickmakers, 10, 0.8; mariners, 8, 0.5; blacksmiths, 7, 0.7; sailmakers, 5, 1.6; goldsmiths, 5, 1.0; butchers, 5, 0.7; carpenters, 5, 0.2; (only groups with 5 or more slaves included).

richest merchants lived on Dock Street, so did many of the slaves. Of the 460 slaves whose place of residence is known, 58 or 12.6 percent lived with Dock Street families. The inhabitants of the section of Queen Street below Wall Street, which was the second most commercially important street held 50 blacks or 10.9 percent of the total, as did the residents of the South Ward section of Broad Street.[17]

Fewer slaves lived in the more modest sections of the city away from the southernmost tip of the island, but 69 did reside in the streets of the East Ward north of Wall Street, and 43 were located on Broadway in the West Ward. The typical white inhabitants of these areas were not well-to-do, and a few wealthy families owned most of the slaves. Abraham De Peyster, a leading merchant who lived in the northern section of the East Ward, owned 9, as did William Smith, another key merchant, who made his home on Broadway.[18]

Bounded by Dock Street, Broad Street, Broadway, and Beaver Street, and also including Pearl Street, the South Ward was the second most well-to-do in the city. Englishmen and Frenchmen were more numerous than the Dutch on several important South Ward blocks, including, as has been noted, Bridge, Dock, and Pearl Streets. But Dutch dominance on Stone

[17] The following notes the number of slaves living on each of Manhattan's major streets: Queen/Smith's Valley, 69; Dock, Dock Ward, 58; Broad, South Ward, 50; Queen, south of Wall, 50; Broadway, 43; Pearl, 22; Stone, 20; Broad, North Ward, 19; Wall, 15; Burger's Path, 12; Crown, 12; Dock, South Ward, 12; Duke, 12; Smith, 10; Beaver, 9; Bridge, 7; Prince, 6; King, 3; Maiden Lane, 3; Marketfield, 3; New, 2; Nassau, 1. Crown, King, and Nassau Streets, and Maiden Lane lay in the northern areas of the North and East Wards. In most of the computations in this study they have been included as parts of the Upper North Ward or of the Smith's Valley.

[18] "Census of the City of New York [About the Year 1703]," *DHNY*, I, 612, 169; De Peyster's property mentioned in New York City, Water Grants, Liber A, pp. 97–101; Smith's location determined by tax lists of Broadway residents.

Street, where they accounted for 11 of the 14 ethnically identifiable residents, helped give them 55 percent of the total population of the district.

Members of old, renowned Dutch families were the core of
the Stone Street community. The widow of the merchant-prince
Oloff Stevensen Van Cortlandt had a home there assessed for
£150 and she paid taxes on another £200 worth of property at
various Manhattan locations. Rip Van Dam, New York's foremost merchant and a member of the Governor's Council from
1702 until 1735, owned a Stone Street house valued at approximately £200. Harmen Rutgers, a brewer whose assessment was
£100, was the son of Rutgers Jacobzsen, who emigrated to Fort
Orange in 1636 and became a wealthy man in the town which
the English renamed Albany. Harmen, who inherited his father's estate, moved to New York City in 1693 in the wake of
Indian raids in the northern part of the colony.[19] Isaac Gouverneur, an aspiring merchant, lived with his mother, whose second husband, the important miller Jasper Nessepatt, had recently died. In 1704, Isaac, whose brother Abraham was a
leader of the Leislerian faction, married Sarah Staats, the
daughter of Samuel Staats, another influential provincial politician.[20]

Dutch citizens filled the middle-ranking and poorer streets
which were located at the center of the settlement. Except in the
affluent section of Queen Street, south of Wall Street, the Dutch

[19] Ernest H. Crosby, *The Rutgers Family of New York* (New York, 1886).
Before the English take-over of New York, the Dutch used their traditional
patronymic system in establishing names; thus Harmen Rutgers [Rutgerzsen]
was the son of Rutgers Jacobzsen. In later years, after New York became an
English colony, the Dutch adopted the system of family names used by the
English. In this way Rutgers became a standard family name.
[20] W. E. De Riemer, *The De Riemer Family* (New York, 1905); E. R.
Purple, ''Grevenraet Family,'' *Contributions to the History of New Amsterdam and New York,* p. 20.

outnumbered the English and French combined on every block of the East, West, and North Wards. The East Ward was bound on the south and west by Smith Street and on the east by the shore. The West Ward was bordered by the Hudson River and by Beaver and New Streets. The North Ward took in the neighborhood situated north of Beaver and Prince Streets and was enclosed on the west by New Street and on the east by Smith Street. The East, West, and North Wards originally had their northern boundaries at Wall Street, but as the city expanded, all three correspondingly extended their uptown limits.

The Dutch comprised 53 percent of the population of the East Ward, which was economically the middle-ranking of New York's five central political districts. They composed 58 percent of the West Ward, and, most strikingly, 78 percent of the persons in the North Ward, the poorest area in the city. The Dutch accounted for 33 of the 36 ethnically identifiable individuals in the North Ward section of Broad Street, which, with a score of 5.1, fit in the middle of the scale of wealth. And they provided 14 of the 15 denizens of New Street, the boundary between the West and North Wards, which scored only 3.5 on the scale. New Street, which had been opened in the 1680s, was the poorest large block in the port.

Adding the 194 people whose ethnic backgrounds have been tentatively identified to the 638 Dutch, English, and French whose nationalities have been definitely ascertained, and then recalculating the composition of the wards only slightly changes the results. The dominance of the English and French in the wealthy Dock Ward becomes more clear, as their proportion of the population rises from 52 percent to 57 percent. In the South Ward, the Dutch percentage rises to 57 percent, and in the East, West, and North, it falls to 51 percent, 53 percent, and 77 percent.

Men engaged in sea-oriented pursuits frequently dwelled in

the houses of the East Ward. Merchants clustered in the English area of Queen Street, but masters, mariners, and shipwrights spread throughout the area. Of the 50 masters known to have had addresses on Manhattan's major streets, 18 lived on Queen Street and 5 more on Smith Street. Of the 25 mariners, 5 lived in the Smith's Valley near the East River north of Wall Street, where most of the houses lay along the upper reaches of Queen Street; 2 more made their dwellings on Queen Street below Wall and another on the east side of Smith Street. Shipwrights also favored the Smith's Valley, and 10 out of 19 were housed there (Table 9).

Seafarers, by necessity mobile men, were often tenants, as were merchants. At least 11 of 31 mariners or 35 percent, 22 of

Table 9. Residential distribution of certain occupations

	Baker	Bolter	Brickmaker	Carman	Carpenter	Cooper	Cordwainer	Gentleman	Mariner	Master	Merchant	Shipwright	Tailor
Upper North Ward	1	0	0	3	3	3	1	1	1	2	1	2	1
New	0	1	4	1	3	0	2	1	0	0	0	1	0
Broadway	1	1	10	4	10	0	6	4	4	6	3	1	2
Broad	2	3	0	1	6	6	2	0	3	7	11	1	0
Wall	1	1	0	0	1	1	3	2	0	1	5	1	0
Queen/Smith's Valley	3	0	1	1	3	2	4	3	5	9	12	10	1
Smith	2	1	1	0	1	1	2	0	1	5	2	0	0
Queen, south of Wall	2	0	0	0	1	2	1	2	2	9	16	1	1
Prince	0	1	0	0	0	1	1	0	2	0	5	0	1
Burger's Path	0	0	0	0	0	0	0	0	0	0	4	0	0
Duke/Mill	1	0	0	0	1	1	2	1	1	2	3	1	0
Dock, Dock Ward	2	1	0	0	1	1	3	0	0	1	16	0	3
Dock, South Ward	0	0	0	0	1	0	0	2	0	1	2	0	0
Pearl	1	1	0	0	3	1	2	1	2	1	8	1	0
Bridge	1	2	0	0	0	0	0	1	1	2	3	0	0
Stone	0	0	0	0	0	1	1	1	1	0	2	0	0
Marketfield	0	0	0	0	1	0	1	0	0	1	0	0	0
Beaver	1	0	0	0	2	0	2	0	2	3	1	0	0
Not specifically located	6	1	8	3	4	4	5	7	6	5	16	2	1
Total	24	13	24	13	41	24	38	26	31	55	110	21	10

Sources: The 1703 assessment list and others mentioned previously

55 masters or 40 percent, and 38 of 110 merchants or 35 percent did not maintain independent residences. The natural desire of these men to be close to the dock area helped make the East Ward the center of tenancy in the city. Of the 254 individuals or heads of families in the East Ward, 119 or 47 percent lived under landlords' roofs. The phenomenon was less frequent in the West and North Wards, where 29 percent and 23 percent of the people were tenants respectively, and was even more rare in the well-to-do Dock and South Wards, where the rates fell to 19 percent and 10 percent respectively.

In addition to those whose employment demanded travel, the tenants included the poor, the widowed, and numbers of young married couples. On the ten-interval scale of relative wealth, tenants scored only 2.42 while landlords scored 6.62 and individual householders 6.39. Besides sea-going pursuits, tenants frequently pursued low-income occupations such as ship carpentry. Of the 21 shipwrights, 10 did not have independent homes. Penury or personal choice led 25 widows, or 18 percent of the 136 in the population under examination, to live with strangers or with their children. However, persons recently wed probably made up the majority of the tenant population in 1703. Of the 180 tenants whose marriage statuses are known, 135 had spouses. Of the 96 tenants whose wedding dates are available, 61 exchanged vows after 1695. These relative newlyweds, who apparently lacked the financial means to set up independent households, were not typical of New York's young married residents; at least 100 couples who wed after 1695 began married life in, or quickly obtained, their own homes.

Numerous tradesmen lived in the West and North Wards. The 10 carmen with addresses known to have been on the city's major streets made their homes in the districts. Out of 20 coopers, 12, including at least 5 on Broad Street, resided in the North Ward. Of 37 carpenters, 10 lived on Broadway, 4 on other West Ward roads, and 9 more on adjacent North Ward streets. Brickmakers, probably drawn to the shore of the Hudson by the availability of the clay necessary to their work, also favored Broadway. Ten of the 16 brickmakers made their homes on this wide western road, another 4 on nearby New Street, and 5 more on other West and North Ward blocks (Table 9).

Residentially, New York City in 1703 clearly reflected the effects of the English conquest of the province. The minority group of English and Huguenot immigrants, who in the course of the last quarter of the seventeenth century captured a controlling share of New York's wealth and commerce, naturally had moved into many of the most luxurious areas. In contrast, large numbers of the Dutch found themselves relegated to more marginal areas. Some Dutch may have escaped this fate by migrating from Manhattan, but the evidence does not indicate that ordinary Dutch residents of the city had any noteworthy success in obtaining country acres.[21]

Of course, rich Dutch citizens lived on the island's fashionable blocks, but the English and French minority formed a majority of the inhabitants of the richest district, the Dock Ward, and made Dock Street the hub of their society. The Dutch accounted for four of every five families in the poorest area, the North Ward, and filled the residences of another recently developed block, New Street, which was one of the poorest in the city.

Many Dutch New Yorkers were frustrated by life in the city in the late seventeenth century. They had gracefully accepted the takeover by the English Crown but they were unwilling to become economic and social inferiors in the community es-

---

[21] Secretary of State, New York State, *Calendar of New York Colonial Manuscripts: Indorsed Land Papers in the Office of the Secretary of State of New York, 1643–1803* (Albany, 1864); New York State, Land Patents, 1680–1751, Vol. VI, New York State Library, Albany.

tablished by their fathers. They could not compete with the English and French, who often enjoyed striking advantages in
commerce, and without access to wealth they could not build
their homes in the most desirable areas of the city. But the
Dutch did have numerical strength and memories, and these
were important when the consequences of the English conquest
began to affect the city's politics.

5 ❧ *Leisler's Rebellion*

New Amsterdam's burghers reacted with remarkable equanimity when the English fleet which had been dispatched to subdue them sailed into their harbor in 1664. To the chagrin of Peter Stuyvesant, the Dutch West India Company governor, the city's leaders decided to surrender the town without firing a shot. They were aware of the unready state of the municipal defenses, but more important, they found strong attraction in the peace terms offered by Colonel Richard Nicolls, the commander of the expedition.[1]

England had no reason to destroy New Amsterdam's prosperity, but only wished to transfer some of its profits to English coffers. Accordingly, Nicolls's terms were generous and were designed to conciliate the Dutch residents and to win their allegiance. The Articles of Capitulation guaranteed to the burghers the uninterrupted possession of their houses, lands, goods, and ships, and allowed them to follow the customs of the Netherlands in the inheritance of estates. The Anglican conquerors prudently chose not to force conformity to the Church of England, but rather assured the Dutch of their right to worship at the Calvinist Reformed Church. Economically, the

[1] "Answer of Ex-Director Stuyvesant . . . 1666;" "Extract of a Letter from the Director-General . . . to the Directors of the West India Company, Chamber at Amsterdam, dated the 4th of August, 1664;" "Director Stuyvesant to the Dutch Towns on Long Island," Aug. 28, 1664; "Answer [of the Dutch Towns]," n.d., *DRNY*, II, 431, 433, 444–45, 505, 376.

Dutch retained many old privileges, and in addition gained the right of trading with England and her colonies. Finally, the English offered the inhabitants political liberties, including the selection of deputies, and promised them that they would not have to bear arms against any foreign nation.[2]

Prospects of peace and prosperity enticed the burghers, who for forty years had conducted their affairs under the erratic leadership of the Dutch West India Company. The conquest bloodlessly terminated the colonists' long-term border disputes with neighboring English provinces and promised to permanently remove the fear of war for the isolated Dutchmen. It also secured them a degree of protection against hostile Indians which the Company had never afforded its settlers.[3] Indeed, the peace seemed to offer the Dutch the opportunity to develop the community for their own benefit rather than for that of the stockholders.

English jurisdiction at first lay lightly on the shoulders of the Dutch, but before long it began to transform the life of the city. Colonel Nicolls, who became the first English governor, changed the names of both New Amsterdam and New Netherland to New York, and on June 12, 1665, he organized all the settlements on Manhattan Island into a city with a corporate frame of government. Nicolls replaced the Dutch system of schout, burgomasters, and schepens with the English one of sheriff, mayor, and aldermen, and retained the authority to appoint these officials annually.[4]

Recapture of New York in 1673 by Dutch forces gave the

[2] "Articles of Capitulation on the Reduction of New Netherland," Aug. 27, 1664, *ibid.,* pp. 251–52.

[3] "Remonstrance of the Burgomasters and Schepens of New Amsterdam, and the Delegates from the Adjoining Towns, to the Honble the Directors of the West India Company, Chamber at Amsterdam, dated 2d November 1663," *ibid.,* pp. 477–79.

[4] "Colonel Nicolls to the Duke of York," n.d., *ibid.,* III, 105; "Nicolls Charter, 1665," June 12, 1665, *DHNY,* I, 602–4.

city's Dutch community an opportunity to express their opinion of English rule. The leaders of the port, which was renamed New Orange, proclaimed "the great joy of the good inhabitants" and promised their undying affection to the States General and the Prince of Orange for liberation from the English. They quickly called attention to the benefits which the city could offer the Netherlands as a refuge for those displaced by war, a granary for the homeland and its colonies, and as a source of beaver, tobacco, and military intelligence. These protestations doubtless were in part pro forma communications of submission expected by the home government, but they were more than simply examples of imperial etiquette. The townsmen, no longer wards of the West India Company or of a foreign monarchy, had become direct subjects of the Netherlands. The joy which they expressed at being united with "their lawfull and native Sovereigns" and with the "Fatherland" seemed genuine, and perhaps reflected their uneasiness with the changes wrought under England's jurisdiction.[5]

Dutch forms and practices soon reappeared in the city. On August 17, 1673, the commanders and council of war, after meeting with six deputies elected by the citizenry, reintroduced the old form of municipal government. They appointed a schout, and chose three burgomasters and five schepens from a list of nominees drawn up by vote of the commoners. Men with Dutch names filled every position: Anthony De Milt became schout, Johannes Van Brugh, Johannes De Peyster, and Egidius Luyck, burgomasters; and William Beeckman, Jeronimus Ebbingh, Jacob Kip, Laurens Vanderspeigle, and Guleyn Verplanck, schepens.[6]

---

[5] "Nathan Gould's Account of the Capture of New York," Aug. 1673; "The Corporation of New Orange to the States-General," Sept. 8, 1673, *DRNY*, III, 201; II, 526–27.

[6] "Minutes of Council of New Netherland, 1673, 1674," Aug. 16, and 17, 1673, *ibid.*, II, 574–75. It is unclear just who was allowed to vote in this election; voters were only identified as members of the commonality.

Whatever were the wishes of its inhabitants, Manhattan was not destined to remain a Dutch possession. By the Treaty of Westminster signed on February 9, 1674, Holland returned the city and colony to England. On November 10, English forces took over the surrendered port, and James Stuart was once again in possession of his proprietary, which was for a second time named New York.[7]

The Duke of York dispatched Edmund Andros to be governor-general of his province. James instructed Andros to encourage men of all nations to settle in New York, but the proprietor was especially anxious that Englishmen be added to the population. Unsure of the allegiance of his subjects, the Duke advised his surrogate to act impartially toward all the inhabitants, but to watch carefully the Dutch who cooperated with the leaders of the capture of the port in 1673. As has been noted, the regime also took action to reduce Dutch influence and to bring the province fully into England's economic orbit by forbidding vessels from the Netherlands to bring goods to New York.[8]

Andros set out immediately to re-establish English authority. He required the Dutch to take an oath of allegiance to the Crown, which, the burgomasters complained, was more harsh than the one imposed on Englishmen during the 1673–1674 Dutch occupation. The Dutch also argued that the new pledge, unlike the one administered by Nicolls in 1664, did not clearly absolve them from the obligation to bear arms against the Netherlands in time of war.[9]

---

[7] "The States-General to Charles II," Dec. 19, 1673; "Report of the Council of Trade . . . respecting the Recapture of New York," Nov. 15, 1673, *ibid.*, II, 531; III, 211–12.

[8] "Commission of Major Edmund Andros to be Governor of New York," July 1, 1674; "Instructions for Governor Andros," July 1, 1674, *ibid.*, III, 215, 216.

[9] "Petition of the Dutch Burghers of New York," Mar. 16, 1675, *ibid.*, II, 740–43.

Governor Andros put into effect in the province the Duke's Laws, a combination of New England codes and common law procedures, and ordered the courts to conduct their business in the English language. In New York City, Andros re-introduced the offices of sheriff, mayor, and alderman. The names of Englishmen naturally began to appear frequently among the office-holders appointed by the governor to direct the affairs of the port. In October 1675 Governor Andros appointed William Dervall mayor of the city, Thomas Gibbs and Thomas Lewis aldermen, and John Sharpe secretary.[10]

Despite the willingness of leading Dutch citizens to cooperate with the authorities, the transition to English forms of government created certain problems. The municipal officers sitting on the Court of Mayor and Aldermen, or Court of Sessions, had special difficulties. English control was stricter, and the judges, unlike their predecessors in the years from 1664 until 1673, kept their records in the language of the victors. But Dutch influence remained and the court continued to follow many procedures from Roman Dutch law. It also attempted to retain, in a manner reminiscent of the Court of Burgomasters, Schepens, and Schout, jurisdiction over criminal and equity matters as well as civil cases.[11]

The greatest problem was the introduction of the English jury system, which caused a crisis in the municipal courts. The judges employed the device in some cases where it was inappropriate and declined to use it in others where it was mandatory. As a result, in 1681 a grand jury composed exclusively of Englishmen indicted several local officials for treason on the

[10] "Order to Put Duke's Laws into Force in New York," Aug. 6, 1674, *ibid.*, III, 226–27; *Min. Com. Coun.*, Oct. 17, 1675, I, 1.

[11] Herbert A. Johnson, "The Advent of Common Law in Colonial New York," in George A. Billias, ed., *Selected Essays: Law and Authority in Colonial America* (Barre, Mass., 1965), pp. 80–82; Richard B. Morris, ed., *Select Cases of the Mayor's Court of New York City, 1674–1874* (Washington, D.C., 1935), pp. 46–47.

grounds that two years earlier they had refused to allow the Englishman John Tuder a trial by jury. These officials included the mayor, François Rombouts, a Huguenot who had emigrated from the Netherlands and had been a successful merchant since the days of New Amsterdam, and the Dutch aldermen William Beeckman, Johannes Van Brugh, Guleyn Verplanck and Peter Jacobs. The General Court of Assizes acquitted the accused, but the city officials were much chastened by the experience.[12]

Common citizens were no more immune than their social superiors from the complications which arose from the meeting of English and Dutch in New York. Even the men of the constable's watch fell prey to hostile ethnic thoughts, with detrimental effects to the peace which they were supposed to preserve. Indeed, in 1676 and again in 1682 the authorities thought it necessary to threaten with punishment those who "shall presume to make any quarrel upon the watch upon the account of being of different nations . . . ."[13]

The advent of Thomas Dongan as governor gave hope for a relaxation of these tensions. Soon after the new governor arrived in New York in August 1683 the mayor and aldermen of the city asked that he confirm the liberties previously exercised by the municipality. They requested, moreover, a number of additional privileges such as popular selection of local officials. Dongan studied the proposals and conditionally granted most of them while he and the town fathers awaited final approval from the proprietor, who became king of England in 1685 upon the death of his brother Charles II. The new monarch, in accord with his earlier predilection to extend to New York City "immunities and priviledges beyond wt other parts of my territoryes

---

[12] "Proceedings of the General Court of Assizes Held in the City of New York, October 6, 1680 to October 6, 1682," *Court Records, 1680–1682, 1693–1701,* in the *Coll. NYHS,* XLV (1912), 9, 13, 22.

[13] *Min. Com. Coun.,* Jan. 11, 1676, Oct. 6, 1682, I, 8, 93.

doe enjoy," agreed to issue a municipal charter which went into effect in 1686.[14]

Despite its generally liberal character, the Dongan Charter placed significant restraints on the city's autonomy. The townsmen had suggested that the governor and his council select the mayor annually from the group of newly elected aldermen, but the charter did not impose this limit upon the executive. Dongan and his successors retained the sole power to appoint New York's chief magistrate and to fill the important posts of recorder and treasurer.[15]

Inhabitants of each of the six wards established by the charter had the right to elect one alderman and one assistant to participate with the mayor in the administration of public affairs. Residents of each district also chose two assessors to evaluate property for purposes of taxation, a collector to receive the moneys levied, and a constable to maintain law and order. These elections took place annually on September 29, the feast of Saint Michael the Archangel, and the successful candidates took office on October 14.[16]

Meeting together every Tuesday, the mayor, recorder, aldermen, and assistants composed the Common Council, which by the charter had full authority to "make Laws, Orders, Ordinances & Constitutions" for the city. In its legislative capacity the Council was active in all aspects of municipal life and growth, including the laying out and the paving of streets, the sale of public land, the erection of buildings, the collection of refuse, and the regulation of certain businesses. Some of the officers also had judicial powers. The mayor, recorder, and aldermen formed a Court of Common Pleas or Mayor's Court,

[14] "Petition of the Mayor and Common Council of New York for a New Charter," Nov. 9, 1683; "Instructions for Governor Dongan," Jan. 27, 1683, *DRNY*, III, 337–39, 334.

[15] *Min. Com. Coun.*, Jan. 5, 1693, I, 290–305.   [16] *Ibid*.

which had civil jurisdiction, and the mayor, recorder, and between three and five aldermen were commissioned as justices of
the peace with minor criminal jurisdiction.[17]

Full implementation of the Dongan Charter might have pre-
vented the turmoil which in a few years was to disturb New
York's politics. The charter took effect at a critical time when
the Dutch were losing economic control of the city but still retained great numerical strength. It authorized the election of
many municipal officeholders and allowed political participation
not only by the Dutch grandees but also by the ambitious, less
well-connected Dutch whose situations more closely resembled
those of the ordinary burghers. Success in local politics might
have appeased the lower echelon Dutch leaders who became so
prominent in the later troubles, and a voice in the affairs of the
city might have made the effects of the English conquest less
galling to the average Dutch resident.

However, James II's decision in 1688 to add the colony of
New York to the newly created Dominion of New England
greatly minimized the positive consequences of the Dongan
Charter. Boston became the regional seat of government, and
New York City became an outpost of a union including Mas-
sachusetts Bay, Plymouth, New Hampshire, the Narragansett
Country, Connecticut, Rhode Island, New York, and East and
West Jersey.

Edmund Andros, a former governor of New York, became
the royal executive of the Dominion, and some of his former
allies from the Hudson River province exerted great power in
the new amalgam. According to disgruntled Massachusetts
leaders, a coterie of eight New Yorkers dominated the 42-man
Council which advised Andros. Even Edward Randolph, a
Crown agent who had little sympathy for Massachusetts politi-

[17] *Ibid.* All sales of public land were made in the name of the mayor, aldermen, and commonality.

cians, complained that "the governor is safe in his New Yorke confidents, all others being strangers to his councill."[18]

The New Yorkers who held power in the Dominion represented the cream of the Dutch and English elite in the city and the colony. Local leaders in Manhattan suffered a relative loss of status, and the Dutch residents of the port became a minority in the population of the union. Charles Lodowyck, a merchant and militia captain, expressed the dissatisfaction of the lower-ranking leaders at this situation. A Dutchman, Lodowyck bitterly reported that Andros's deputy, Captain Francis Nicholson, who took over the administration of New York province, declared that "we here meaning the Inhabitants of this Government, could but account ourselves as a conquered people. . . ."[19]

England's Glorious Revolution of 1688 soon brought an end to the Dominion of New England. In Massachusetts the government had been an imposed agency controlled by outsiders who irked the Bay Colony's property owners and merchants by closely examining land titles and by reserving the choicest patronage for themselves. Andros aggravated the situation by putting pressure on the Puritans to erect and support an Anglican chapel. The Boston leadership was united in opposition to the Dominion, and as soon as news of the deposition of James II reached the city, they arrested Andros and overthrew the government.[20]

New York's leadership, on the other hand, was seriously

[18] Bernard Bailyn, *The New England Merchants in the Seventeenth Century* (Cambridge, Mass., 1955), p. 176; Michael G. Hall, *Edward Randolph and the American Colonies* (Chapel Hill, N.C., 1960), p. 158.

[19] "Charles Lodowyck's Deposition concerning Governor Nicholson," July 25, 1689, *Documents Relating to the Administration of Leisler,* in the *Coll. NYHS,* I (1868), 295.

[20] Herbert Levi Osgood, *The American Colonies in the Eighteenth Century* (New York, 1924), III, 415–23.

divided. The most important residents had been influential in the Andros regime and their continued loyalty to it after his fall spurred men of less renown, who had experienced only frustration under the Dominion, to challenge their right to rule. The ensuing struggle fed upon the ethnic and social divisions within the community as each group sought popular affirmation for its claim, and the outcome spawned a generation of conflict and recrimination.

Lieutenant Governor Francis Nicholson and New York City's Dominion councilors Nicholas Bayard, Anthony Brockholst, Frederick Philipse, and Stephen Van Cortlandt learned on March 1, 1689 that the Prince of Orange had landed in England to seize the throne. Their position was precarious. If they proclaimed William as the new king and he failed to gain his objective, they would be liable to charges of treason. If they reaffirmed their allegiance to James and he proved unable to hold the crown, they could lose their offices, property, and lives. Speaking out could only imperil them, so they chose to suppress the news and to await developments silently.[21]

Word of Andros's arrest by the Massachusetts magistrates reached New York on April 26 and rumors of war with France came the following day. No longer able to maintain their silence the lieutenant governor and the councilors, including Van Cortlandt who was also mayor, revealed the truth to the aldermen and assistants. Together they made a fateful decision on April 29 to strengthen the city's defenses by having each of the militia companies, on a rotating schedule, provide supplemental guards for Fort James, located at the southern tip of Manhattan.[22]

Events stabilized until the end of May when a crisis of ill-will and misunderstanding suddenly developed. On his own initia-

---

[21] "Stephen Van Cortlandt to Governor Andros," July 9, 1689, *DRNY*, III, 591.

[22] *Ibid*.

tive militia lieutenant Henry Cuyler attempted to station a sentry at the sally port of the fort. Irked by this intrusion on his tactical control of the fort, Lieutenant Governor Nicholson reasserted his authority and railed at Cuyler that he "rather would see the Towne on fire than to be commanded by you." Many among the citizenry interpreted Nicholson's deprecatory response as a threat to burn the town or to betray it to the enemy, and the more rash decided to take action. On the afternoon of May 31, a large number of people gathered in front of the house of militia leader Jacob Leisler and marched to the fort, where Cuyler admitted them.[23]

While his men stood guard at Fort James on June 3, Captain Leisler, who claimed to have received word of a cluster of unidentified ships off Sandy Hook, Long Island, sounded the alarm to summon the other militia units. When the soldiers arrived, they were invited into the fort. There they agreed to and signed "A Declaration of the Inhabitants Soldiers Belonging under the Severall Companies of the Train Band of New York," pledging themselves to hold the fortress in trust for William and Mary.[24]

Nicholson's response was to slip away from the city and sail home to England on June 10. In the next two months Leisler consolidated his hold on the rebellion. On June 22, he read in front of the fort an official announcement of the accession of William and Mary, and he then demanded that Mayor Van

[23] *Ibid.*, p. 577.

[24] "A Modest and Impartial Narrative of Social Grievances and Great Oppressions That Peaceable and Most Considerable Inhabitants of Their Majesties Province of New York in America Lye Under, By the Extravagant and Arbitrary Proceedings of Jacob Leisler and His Accomplices," Jan. 21, 1690, *ibid.*, p. 670; "A Declaration of the Inhabitants Soldiers," May 31, 1689, *DHNY*, II, 10. Charles McLean Andrews attributed "A Modest and Impartial Narrative" to Nicholas Bayard (*Narratives of the Insurrections, 1675–1690* [New York, 1915], p. 319).

Cortlandt proclaim the new monarchs at City Hall. Van Cortlandt declined, lamely arguing that the captain had already made
public the decree. The mayor's hesitation made the old leadership vulnerable to Leisler's immediate charges of treason and
popery, and ended all possibility of halting the revolt. At the
end of June, Leisler rid himself of the bothersome municipal
government by cautioning the aldermen against holding a
Mayor's Court session scheduled for July 2; the frightened
judges heeded the warning and did not meet again for almost
two years.[25]

A Committee of Safety composed of the insurgent leadership
named Leisler captain of the fort on June 8 and on August 16
declared him to be commander in chief of the province. In
December, Leisler took possession of instructions which arrived
from King William addressed "To our Trusty and welbeloved
Francis Nicholson Esquire and Lieut. Governor and Commander
in Chief our Province of New York in America and in his absence to such as for the time being take care for Preserving the
Peace and administring the Lawes in our said Province of New
York in America." The letter authorized the recipient "to take
upon you the Government of the said Province," and Leisler
thereafter styled himself Lieutenant Governor.[26]

Jacob Leisler was a predictable type of leader for this insurgency. The circumstances naturally thrust forward a man
who had once been near the center of power in the province but
in later days had found himself more often at its edges. Leisler
had long feuded with the ruling clique, and he had a self-serving
mental outlook which enabled him to equate his personal foes
with the enemies of God.

[25] "Van Cortlandt to Andros," 595–96.

[26] "Commission from the Committee of Safety Appointing Jacob Leisler to
be Captain of the Fort," June 8, 1689; "Commission to Captain Leisler to be
Commander in Chief," Aug. 16, 1689, *DHNY*, II, 11, 23; "William III to
Lieutenant Governor Nicholson," July 30, 1689, *DRNY*, III, 606.

As a marginal leader, locally prominent but without real power, Leisler resembled the spokesmen of other late seventeenth century uprisings against colonial administrations. The similarities between prominent Leislerians, key figures of Nathaniel Bacon's rebellion in Virginia, the coterie around John Coode in Maryland, and those Massachusetts merchants who supported the revocation of the Bay Colony's charter are noteworthy. But generalizations which classify these phenomena as clashes between competing elites are not sufficient. Any analysis which focuses on the leadership of the forces involved in a political conflict will inevitably produce a description of a divided elite, and usually members of one of the contending groups will emerge as "peripheral" or "marginal."

The differences between Leisler and the other rebels of the late seventeenth century are more important than their similarities. Nathaniel Bacon was a young man who found his hopes of making a fortune thwarted by the vested interest of Virginia's already sated leadership. John Coode was an ambitious Protestant latecomer to Maryland, who in pursuing his dream of success ran afoul of an entrenched Catholic elite. Massachusetts's merchants had already gained economic dominance in the province, but found their path to political control blocked by the old Puritan leadership.[27]

Jacob Leisler was not a man on the way up who found an older group of leaders impeding his progress. He was a representative of an earlier elite which latecomers had bypassed.

[27] Wilcomb E. Washburn, *The Governor and the Rebel: A History of Bacon's Rebellion in Virginia* (Chapel Hill, N.C., 1957), pp. 17, 18; Bernard Bailyn, "Politics and Social Structure in Virginia," in James M. Smith, ed., *Seventeenth-Century America* (Chapel Hill, N.C., 1959), p. 103; Michael G. Kammen, "The Causes of the Maryland Revolution of 1689," *Maryland Historical Magazine,* LV (Dec. 1960), 293–324; Lois Green Carr and David William Jordan, *Maryland's Revolution of Government, 1689–1692* (Ithaca, N.Y., 1974), ch. 1; Bailyn, *New England Merchants,* ch. 7.

Leisler's status had fallen because his affiliations with the Dutch were no longer of use in a colony owned by the English.

Born in Frankfurt am Main in 1640, Leisler migrated to New Amsterdam as a twenty-year-old soldier with the Dutch West India Company. He was the son of a minister, Jacob Victorius Leyssler, the Calvinist pastor of Bockenheim, and probably grew up in a more substantial situation than his modest status upon arrival in America implied. The Leysslers sent Jacob's brother to the University of Geneva, which indicates that the family enjoyed at least a modicum of economic success as well as the social prestige associated with the ministry.[28]

On April 11, 1663, Leisler established himself as one of the city's most notable residents by marrying Elsje Tymens, the widow of the wealthy merchant, Pieter Cornelisen Van der Veen. The marriage provided him with capital to trade in furs, tobacco, and wines, and he soon gained a place among the community's most affluent members. During the Dutch reoccupation in 1673–1674 Leisler's estate was assessed at 15,000 florins, making him the sixth richest man in town.[29]

Through his marriage Leisler became an in-law of the foremost families in the province, including the Loockermans, Bayards, and Van Cortlandts. An ambitious latecomer with tenuous connections to the elite, Leisler managed to reach the pe-

[28] Stanley M. Pargellis, "Jacob Leisler," *Dictionary of American Biography* (New York, 1933), VI, 156–57; Edwin Ruthven Purple, *Genealogical Notes Relating to Lieut.-Gov. Jacob Leisler and His Family Connections in New York* (New York, 1877), p. 7; Charles W. Baird, "The Birthplace and Parentage of Jacob Leisler," *Magazine of American History,* II (Aug. 1878), 94.

[29] Purple, *Genealogical Notes . . . Leisler,* p. 7; Pargellis, "Jacob Leisler," pp. 156–57; James Grant Wilson, *The Memorial History of the City of New York* (New York, 1893), I, 129. Only Frederick Philipse (80,000), Cornelius Steenwyck (50,000), Nicholas De Meyer (50,000), Oloff Stevensen Van Cortlandt (45,000), and Jeronimus Ebbingh (30,000) had more florins than Leisler.

riphery but not the center of the colonial power structure. Doubtless his contentious personality alienated his in-laws and slowed his progress. When Govert Loockermans, his wife's stepfather, died without a will in 1671, the newcomer engaged the Bayards and the Van Cortlandts in extended litigation for possession of the estate. By 1689 the outcome still remained in doubt, but Leisler had gained control of the Loockerman lands on Manhattan.[30]

Calvinist by birth and belief, Leisler felt little charity for less rigorous Protestants and none for Catholics. He often perceived tendencies toward heterodoxy in his personal adversaries. Leisler displayed this ability to combine motives as early as 1675 when he accused of heresy an Albany minister, Nicholas Van Rensselaer, with whose family he was feuding. Van Rensselaer, though serving a Dutch Reformed congregation, had been ordained in England by the Anglican Bishop of Salisbury.[31]

Despite these conflicts, Leisler played a continuing role in public affairs. He served as a mediator in the legal system of New Amsterdam and as a deacon of the Reformed Church. During the Dutch reoccupation of 1673–1674, Leisler was apparently close to Governor Anthony Colve, who placed him on a five-man commission to assess the estates of Manhattan's most affluent citizens for tax purposes.[32] His relationship with

[30] Purple, *Genealogical Notes . . . Leisler,* pp. 7, 32; Purple, "Varleth Family," *Contributions to the History of Ancient Families of New Amsterdam and New York* (New York, 1881), pp. 111–12; L. Effingham De Forest, *The Van Cortlandt Family* (New York, 1930), p. 4; Mariana Griswold (Mrs. Schuyler) Van Rensselaer, *History of the City of New York in the Seventeenth Century* (New York, 1909), II, 370, 470.

[31] Van Rensselaer, *History of New York,* II, 182–85.

[32] Lawrence H. Leder, "Jacob Leisler and the New York Rebellion of 1689–1691" (Master's thesis, New York University, 1950), p. 3; Edwin T. Corwin and Hugh Hastings, eds., *Ecclesiastical Records of the State of New York* (Albany, 1901), II, 800; Wilson, *Memorial History,* I, 129.

the English authorities was not strong, but he remained locally prominent as the captain in command of one of the island's six companies of militia.

Leisler, like other local leaders who were not close associates of Governor Andros, suffered a loss of influence under the Dominion of New England. He resented the new government and during his rebellion wrote disparagingly to England of its narrow distribution of political power. Characteristically he came to see the New Yorkers who supported the Dominion as hypocrites "who under the appearance of the functions of the Protestant Religion, remain still affected to the Papist." [33] Leisler was convinced that his opponents were engaged in a plot against God and King, and he equated his own success with the salvation of true Christianity in New York.

Various considerations, including allegiance to relatives, motivated Leisler's aides. Jacob Milborne, who stood at Leisler's side in the heresy controversy over Van Rensselaer, returned from a voyage to Europe in August 1689 and joined the rebellion. A widower, he married the captain's daughter Mary the following year. Milborne, whose Baptist beliefs differed from those of New York's Anglican establishment, had occasionally clashed with the provincial government, and had once successfully sued Andros in England for false arrest. Samuel Edsall, Milborne's former father-in-law, served as Queens County's representative to Leisler's council, and his connection with the rebel commander may have gained his three sons-in-law, Benjamin Blagge, Pieter De La Noy, and William Lawrence, their seats in that body. [34]

[33] "Lieutenant Governor Leisler and Council to the Bishop of Salisbury," Jan. 7, 1690; "Captain Leisler to King William and Queen Mary," Aug. 20, 1689, *DRNY,* III, 654–55, 615.

[34] Purple, *Genealogical Notes . . . Leisler,* p. 12; Osgood, *American Colonies,* III, 459; Van Rensselaer, *History of New York,* II, 241; Hamilton Fish, *Anthon Genealogy* (New York, 1930), pp. 55–56.

Despite the participation of a few Englishmen, the leadership of the rebellion was unmistakably Dutch. Judging by those who stood trial with Captain Leisler when the rebellion collapsed in 1691, his closest associates were all Dutch. Usually survivors or descendants of New Amsterdam, these men found it difficult or impossible to adjust to the new social order which developed in the aftermath of the English conquest of the city.

Pieter De La Noy, New York's only elected mayor prior to the nineteenth century and a member of Leisler's council, emigrated from Haarlem in the Netherlands and in 1680 married Elizabeth De Potter, the widow of Isaac Bedlow, a member of an old New Amsterdam family. After being widowed he later married the daughter of Samuel Edsall. Abraham Gouverneur, born in 1671 and the town clerk during the revolt, was the son of Nicholas Gouverneur, a prominent Netherlands merchant who had traded with New Amsterdam. The young man's mother, Machteldt De Riemer, was the daughter of an established Manhattan family and remained a resident of the island after the English conquest. The physician Samuel Staats, who also served on Leisler's council, was the classic example of a New Netherlander drawn to the rebellion. The son of Major Abraham Staats, Samuel left the colony when the English arrived in 1664 and returned only after the Prince of Orange landed in England.[35]

But the existence of this "peripheral elite" does not explain the broad-based support for its challenge to authority. Ordinary citizens will respond to such a call only to the extent that they have grievances which are congruent with those of the dissident principals. Leisler's Rebellion succeeded because it strongly appealed to the mass of the Dutch population of New York City.

[35] Fish, *Anthon Genealogy,* pp. 55–56; W. E. De Riemer, *The De Riemer Family* (New York, 1905), pp. 7–8; Jonathan Pearson, "Staats Genealogy," *NYGB Rec.,* II (July 1871), 140–41.

Nicholas Bayard, who fared well under the English regime and
became the chief antagonist of Leisler and his followers during
and after the uprising, persistently claimed that the insurgents
were merely "a parcel of ignorant and innocent people, almost
none but of the Dutch nation." Leisler won their support, according to Bayard, with assurances that William would end English administrative control of New York and would directly
control the colony as his own Dutch fief. Bayard's hatred of the
rebel leader probably distorted his outlook, but he did have an
insight into the nature of the conflict. Indeed, Leisler had even
chosen Fort Amsterdam as the new name of the stronghold at
the southern tip of the island. Leisler was sensitive to these
charges and tried to deny them, but all indications, including
even the sharp decline in participation at the Reformed Church
following the pastor's denunciation of the captain, show deep
Dutch involvement in the revolt.[36]

The accession of the Prince of Orange had inspired Dutch
New Yorkers and led them to reassert themselves. This took the
form of a dual uprising, in defense of certain unassailable institutions, but against some of the persons most closely associated
with their support.[37] In Leisler's Rebellion, Dutch New Yorkers, members of a Reformed church, overthrew their English
Anglican government in the name of the English crown and its
Episcopal religion, a seeming paradox made rational by their af-
fectionate identification with the new monarch. In regard to the

[36] "Colonel Bayard's Narrative of Occurrences in New York, From April
to December, 1689," Dec. 13, 1689, *DRNY,* III, 639; "Leisler's Proclama-
tion Confirming the Election by the Citizens of the Mayor, Sheriff, Clerke,
and Common Council of New York," Oct. 14, 1689; "A Memoriall of What
Has Occurred in Their Maties Province of New York Since the News of Their
Majties Happy Arrivall in England," n.d., *DHNY,* II, 35, 58.

[37] George F. Rudé, *The Crowd in History: A Study of Popular Disturbances
in France and England, 1730–1848* (New York, 1964), ch. 9, discusses similar phenomena.

basic issues, the opponents were in fact indistinguishable. Indeed, the inability of the contending factions, the Leislerians and the Anti-Leislerians, to identify themselves except by reference to the protagonist suggests that they found difficulty in defining their differences. Despite mutual accusation of hypocrisy, both groups shared an allegiance to the Glorious Revolution and Protestantism.

The existence of serious divisions among the city's leaders gave colonial New Yorkers a rare opportunity to choose their spokesmen rather than to defer to the wishes of a unified, recognized elite, and thus the rebellion began. It was the product not of a conspiracy to restore Dutch rule, but rather of the resentment of the many Dutch citizens who had not been able to succeed within the new English order. Leisler and his followers appealed to those longing for older, better days.

Leisler tried to bring all opponents of the Dominion of New England under his aegis. Although he reserved commissions as justices of the peace, sheriffs, and militia officers almost exclusively for Dutchmen in New York City and the communities of the Hudson Valley north to Albany, Leisler frequently offered Englishmen similar positions on Long Island. But despite his claims to a provincial domain, Leisler's power did not extend far beyond the community. The residents of Albany and Kingston scornfully rejected early overtures to join the movement, and the former submitted to Leisler's authority only after the Indian massacre at nearby Schenectady early in 1690. Relatively unaffected by the English conquest, Albany and Kingston had little reason to be attracted to Leisler. Few English immigrants had gone to those river towns, and the old elites were able to retain their positions and the loyalty of the homogeneous populations.[38]

[38] "List of the Commissions Issued by Lt. Govr. Leisler," Dec. 12, 1689 to Jan. 20, 1691, *DHNY*, II, 347–54; David S. Lovejoy, *The Glorious Revolu-*

Leisler's control over Long Island and the Hudson Valley was in fact more titular than effective. He did not maintain sustained communications with the predominantly English anti-Dominion insurgents on Long Island, who looked more to Boston than to Manhattan for direction. As lieutenant governor Leisler did not even appoint a councilor from the eastern end of Long Island, and at the western end in Queens County he faced an uprising led by the Englishman, Major Thomas Willett, in June 1690. Leisler did name William Lawrence and Thomas Williams to his council from Orange and Westchester Counties respectively, but neither of these less developed areas seems to have contributed substantially to the uprising.[39]

Leisler's Rebellion lacked that aspect of the other uprisings of the late seventeenth century which made them in part efforts to guarantee the rights of Englishmen to American colonists. Leisler corresponded with Coode, but their letters show little except a common fear of Catholics. Leisler's attempts to organize an intercolonial military program appear to be only practical steps taken to protect his own endangered province.[40]

Captain Leisler's failure to enunciate clearly his advocacy of the rights of Englishmen was not the result of the unfortunate absence of an able propagandist. Rather his silence reflected the foreignness of the concept to his thinking. Leisler did revive the colonial assembly, whose short life James II had abruptly ended, but he acted reluctantly and only when he desperately needed support for raising revenues. When the delegates broached the subject of English liberties, Leisler prorogued the

---

tion in America, 1660–1692 (New York, 1972), pp. 312–14; Alice P. Kenney, "Dutch Patricians in Colonial Albany," *New York History,* XLIX (July 1968), 249–83.

[39] Lovejoy, *Glorious Revolution,* pp. 322–23; "Appointment of Leisler's Council," Dec. 11, 1689, *DHNY,* II, 45.

[40] Lovejoy, *Glorious Revolution,* p. 284.

first session, and he rejected a bill which the second session passed to secure such rights.[41]

In fact, almost all the New Yorkers who had led the 1680s quest to guarantee the rights of Englishmen to the colony's inhabitants opposed the insurgency. Most of them were Englishmen, as indeed were as many as twelve of the eighteen members of the original colonial assembly of 1683. Only one survivor of that ill-fated gathering, which endorsed the Charter of Liberties and set up English land and court systems in the province, supported Leisler.[42]

"Papist" was Leisler's favorite epithet, but few of these resided in New York at the time. Despite rumors that 200 Catholic soldiers intent on massacring Protestants had taken up positions on nearby Staten Island, the only Romanist troops in the city at this time were two regulars stationed at Fort Amsterdam. In 1696, Governor Benjamin Fletcher reported that only 10 Catholics lived within the bounds of the municipality.[43]

Lacking Catholics, the Leislerians directed their wrath at their English Protestant neighbors, who were logically their allies. The rich merchants and affluent tradesmen of that group who were hostile to the uprising earned special scorn. Bands of rebels beat John Crooke and Edward Taylor, and Lieutenant Governor Leisler from time to time had arrested or seized the goods of Robert Allison, Thomas Clarke, Philip French, Wil-

[41] *Ibid.*, p. 33. Lovejoy argues that Leisler was part of this quest to secure the rights of Englishmen. See also John Murrin, "English Rights as Ethnic Aggression: The English Conquest, the Charter of Liberties of 1683, and Leisler's Rebellion in New York" (Paper presented at American Historical Association Convention, San Francisco, 1973), p. 13.

[42] Murrin, "English Rights," p. 13.

[43] "Affadavit against Col. Bayard and Certain Parties on Staten Island," Sept. 25, 1689, *DHNY*, II, 28–30; "Colonel Bayard's Narrative;" "Names of the Roman Catholics in the City of New York," June 13, 1696, *DRNY*, III, 640; IV, 166.

liam Merritt, John Merritt, and William Nicolls. The insurgents rarely left the confines of New York City, but they did break into the house of Daniel Whitehead, a Queens County justice of the peace.[44]

Frenchmen and renegade Dutch burghers who associated closely with the English or held positions of trust within the government also received harsh treatment. Leisler's men allegedly commandeered seven full and six half-barrels of gunpowder belonging to Gabriel Minvielle, a native of Bordeaux who was mayor of New York for the 1684–1685 term. The lieutenant governor arrested Jacob De Kay and Brandt Schuyler, both representatives of wealthy Dutch families, and Dirck Vanderburgh, a Dutch mason who later became a member of Trinity Church. Leisler treated the vitriolic Nicholas Bayard with reciprocal hostility and kept him in prison for several months.[45]

Jacob Leisler held power in New York for almost two years, but he could not maintain his quasi-executive status indefinitely. On January 4, 1690, William and Mary commissioned a new governor, Colonel Henry Sloughter, a professional soldier. Perhaps acting under the influence of Francis Nicholson, who received the post of lieutenant governor of Virginia as a reward for his services in the Dominion of New England, the monarchs filled the New York Council with men unfriendly to the rebellion, including Nicholas Bayard, Gabriel Minvielle, William Nicolls, Frederick Philipse, and Stephen Van Cortlandt.[46]

[44] "A Modest and Impartial Narrative," pp. 681–82.

[45] "At a Council Held at Fort William Henry," Apr. 13, 1691, *DHNY*, II, 371; Purple, "Varleth Family," p. 89; "A Modest and Impartial Narrative;" "Governor Sloughter to Lord Nottingham," May 6, 1691, *DRNY*, III, 673, 760; Con. Lib., May 13, 1686, XIII, 225–26; Min. Ves., p. 46.

[46] "Draft of a Commission for Henry Sloughter, Esquire, to be Governor of New York, and Order in Council Thereupon," Jan. 4, 1690; "Instructions for

Governor Sloughter and Major Richard Ingoldsby (also spelled Ingoldesby), the commander of two royal infantry companies dispatched to New York by the king, set sail from England on December 1, 1689. Winter storms buffeted the ships near the Bermudas, and the governor's vessel, the *Archangel* suffered damage on the rocks. The crippled man-of-war sought refuge in the islands, but the three remaining craft sailed on and reached New York late in January. Taking it upon himself to reduce the colony in Sloughter's absence, Ingoldsby immediately demanded possession of the city's fort, but Leisler refused to surrender to a major who was unable to produce official orders.[47]

Tension increased as both parties awaited the new governor, and Leisler accused Ingoldsby of having "fomented and invented distinctions among his Majesty's Subjects of the English and Dutch Nations, whereby woeful divisions have arisen to a degree of hate that threatens the destruction of each other." The rebel leader complained of the "Implacable malice and Violence" of his detractors, who "encouraged and protected avowed Papists in arms," and declared the "Major his evil councillors and all their confederates to be enemies to God, their present Majesties and the peace and welfare of this people and Province."[48]

Pushed beyond his endurance, Leisler on March 17 ordered his men in the fort to fire on the approximately five hundred soldiers and militiamen from nearby communities whom Ingoldsby

Colonel Henry Sloughter, Governor of New York," Jan. 31, 1689, *DRNY,* III, 623, 685.

[47] "Governor Sloughter to Lord Nottingham," pp. 340–45; "Leisler's Protest against Major Ingoldesby," Jan. 31, 1691, *DHNY,* II, 320–21.

[48] "Declaration of Leisler and His Party against Major Ingoldesby and His Council," Mar. 16, 1691, *DHNY,* II, 340–45.

had drawn together in the town. A civilian laborer, Josiah Browne, fell dead, and seven of his fellow New Yorkers and one of the king's soldiers were wounded.[49]

Henry Sloughter finally reached New York on March 19 and swore in his councilors, except for Nicholas Bayard and William Nicolls whom the rebels held in their jail. He sent Major Ingoldsby to demand again the surrender of the fort, but Leisler delayed. He dispatched Ensign Joost Stool to make sure that Sloughter had arrived; this young militiaman knew the new governor from the court of William and Mary where he, despite his poor knowledge of English, had served as the insurgents' envoy. After Stool confirmed Sloughter's presence, Leisler sent Jacob Milborne and Pieter De La Noy to discuss the terms of the capitulation. The new governor, however, refused to engage in negotiations which would constitute quasi recognition of Leisler's authority, and instead arrested the emissaries.[50]

On the following day, Ingoldsby, supported by the presence of Sloughter's man-of-war in the harbor, again approached the fort and requested its surrender. When he offered amnesty to all the rebels except the ringleaders, the nearly four hundred men inside laid down their weapons and deserted. The major then entered the fort and took Leisler and his councilors into custody.[51]

Soon after, a grand jury indicted Jacob Leisler, Jacob Milborne, Pieter De La Noy, Abraham Gouverneur, and Geradus Beeckman for murder and treason; Samuel Edsall, Abraham Brazier, Mindert Coerten, Johannes Vermilje, and Thomas Wil-

[49] "Governor Sloughter to Lord Nottingham," p. 760; Lawrence H. Leder, ed., "Records of the Trials of Jacob Leisler and His Associates," *New-York Historical Society Quarterly*, XXVI (Oct. 1952), 449–50.

[50] "Governor Sloughter to Lord Nottingham;" "Governor Sloughter to the Committee," May 7, 1691, *DRNY*, III, 759–60, 762–63.

[51] "Governor Sloughter to the Committee," May 7, 1691, *ibid.*, pp. 766–67.

liams for treason; and several others for riot. On March 26, Governor Sloughter commissioned a court of oyer and terminer composed entirely of Englishmen to conduct the trials. The judges demanded that the defendants speak in English and abused at least one of the men accused of riot for answering in Dutch. When the defendant complained that the requirement was unfair and asked for an interpreter, the Dutch grandee Stephen Van Cortlandt allegedly translated his statement to the court "in a very mischievous, false and perverted manner." [52]

Captain Leisler denied the jurisdiction of the justices and refused to plead until the king passed judgment on the legality of his seizure of control of the colony. His son-in-law Milborne also chose to remain silent, but all the other defendants denied their guilt. Edsall and his son-in-law De La Noy convinced the jurors of their innocence, but the court sentenced Gouverneur to death by hanging for murdering Josiah Browne by shooting him in the chest. The jurors also declared Leisler, Milborne, and Beeckman guilty of murder and treason; Brazier, Coerten, Vermilje, and Williams guilty of treason; and condemned all seven to the usual punishment reserved for traitors. The prisoners were ordered "hanged by the Neck and being Alive their bodys be Cutt Downe to the Earth, that their Bowells be taken out and they being Alive burnt before their faces that their heads shall be struck off and their Bodyes Cutt in four parts and which shall be Deposed of as their Majties Shall Assigne." Governor Sloughter granted most of the prisoners reprieves and admitted them to bail, but he ordered Leisler and Milborne to be executed by hanging and decapitation on May 17, 1691.[53]

---

[52] Leder, ed., "Records of the Trials," p. 436; "Anonymous Deposition of a Defendant," n.d., *Documents Relating to the Administration of Leisler,* in the *Coll. NYHS,* I (1868), 313.

[53] Leder, ed., "Records of the Trials," pp. 440–42, 445–48, 452; "Intended Letter of Governor Sloughter to Secretary Blathwayt," July 1691, *DRNY,* III, 789.

Leisler's Rebellion almost undid the social fabric of New York City, and the vengeance sought by his enemies was a measure of their fright. The rebellion had its roots in the individual and group frustrations which developed from the changes wrought in the municipality during English rule. Unfortunately, Leisler's successes did not retrieve the happy past which history had stolen, and his ultimate failure bequeathed only intensified antagonisms to the future.

6 ∽ Ethnic Politics

Jacob Leisler's execution momentarily restored stability to New York City's politics, but his death could not alter the divisions which separated its residents. Leisler's enemies held firm control of the colony during most of the 1690s, but the arrival of the Earl of Bellomont as governor in 1698 revitalized the rebels. During Bellomont's short tenure, the Anti-Leislerians and the Leislerians again struggled for power. The contest culminated, after the governor's death, in the disputed New York City elections of 1701, which demonstrated the critically important relationship between national background and political allegiance in Manhattan.

The early 1690s marked the completion of the English conquest of New York. The failure of Leisler discredited the Dutch who opposed the new order, and in the aftermath of the rebellion the English were able to translate their growing numerical and economic strength into firm control of the city. While Leisler's disciples remained under restraint, the English leaders took from the government major economic benefits for themselves and their allies and made the Anglican Church the legal religious establishment. Tensions between ordinary English and Dutch citizens relaxed, and the English influence pervaded the city's institutions.

Colonel Sloughter died suddenly on July 23, 1691, and after several months during which Ingoldsby ruled, Benjamin Fletcher became governor in August 1692. Like his predecessors the new executive was unsympathetic to the rebels. During Fletcher's tenure, which lasted until 1698, the Anti-Leislerians seized the spoils of victory, and the governor became infamous for his huge land grants to his friends. Councilors Nicholas Bayard, William Pinhorne, and William Smith, along with Captain Richard Evans of H.M.S. *Richmond,* the Reverend Godfrey Dellius of Albany, and others received a total of more than one million acres, and several more administration supporters each obtained at least a thousand acres.[1]

Leisler's closest associates spent the early years of the 1690s in the shadow of the scaffold. Young Jacob Leisler had to go to England to beseech the Privy Council to restore his father's confiscated estates, and in New York, the provincial legislature threatened the Leislerians with financial ruin by authorizing their opponents to sue for damages suffered during the insurrection. Governor Fletcher used the death sentences which hung over the paroled Leislerian leaders, Gerardus Beeckman, Abraham Brazier, Mindert Coerten, Abraham Gouverneur, Johannes Vermilje, and Thomas Williams, as a means of keeping them politically inactive. When some of them were chosen for the general assembly, in 1693, the governor nullified their election, and he so frequently threatened them with revocation of parole and immediate execution that the harrassed Leislerians eventually petitioned the king for a full pardon as their only guarantee of safety.[2]

Fletcher's tactics helped make his administration a time of

[1] "An Act for the Vacateing Breaking and Annulling Several Extravagant Grants of Land Made by Coll. Fletcher the Late Govr. of This Province under His Majesty," May 16, 1699, *Col. Laws,* pp. 412–13.

[2] For good examples, see "Petition of Jacob Leisler to the King," n.d.; "Abstract of Governor Fletcher's Letter to Mr. Blathwayt," Oct. 5, 1693, *DRNY,* III, 825–26; IV, 54–55; "G. Beekman and M. Coerten to Nicholas Collen," Sept. 24, 1693, *Documents Relating to the Administration of Leisler,* in the *Coll. NYHS,* I (1868), pp. 334–35.

relative calm in the city's politics. Under his governorship, New York mayors, who in the period from March 1691 until October 1711 spent an average of only 1.85 terms in office, enjoyed longer tenures. Although he supported the Anti-Leislerians, Fletcher used his power to appoint the mayor to conciliate Manhattan's political factions. He kept Abraham De Peyster in the post for the three terms between September 1691 and 1694. The De Peysters, unlike most of the great Dutch families who had fared well under the English, had associated themselves with Leisler. Nevertheless, their wealth and mercantile fame distinguished them from the typical Leislerians and made Abraham De Peyster a safe choice for mayor. A year after De Peyster left office, Fletcher appointed an Anti-Leislerian William Merritt to the post. An English merchant who came to New York in 1671, Merritt also retained the office for three years.[3]

Aldermanic tenures, which in the period from March 1691 until October 1711 averaged 3.18 terms, were also longer under Fletcher. Brandt Schuyler, a member of an established Dutch mercantile family which opposed Leisler, won the seven elections in the South Ward between 1691 and 1696. William Beeckman, leader of a famous New Amsterdam family which cooperated in the rebellion, was victorious six times in the East Ward between 1691 and 1695, and Robert Darkins, an English sea captain, accomplished the same feat in the West Ward. Before he became mayor, William Merritt served the Dock Ward for four terms between March 1691 and 1694, and his successor Jacobus Van Cortlandt, another of the Anti-Leislerian Dutch grandees, was alderman for three years.[4]

Relations between ordinary Dutch and English also improved

---

[3] *Min. Com. Coun.*, Oct. 14, 1691; Sept. 29, 1692, 1693, 1695, 1696; Oct. 14, 1697, I, 238, 286, 333, 382, 423; II, 17.

[4] *Ibid.*, Mar. 29, 1691; Sept. 29, 1691, 1692, 1693, 1694, 1695, 1696, I, 214, 236, 286, 332, 366, 381, 422. There were two elections in 1691.

in the early 1690s. Bereft of leaders able to stir national consciousness, at least some Dutch residents found themselves at ease with the English, and the frequency of intermarriage rose to a level unmatched in the preceding or following years. Of the 24 Dutch residents of the city who were wed in the Reformed Church in 1694, 7 took English spouses. In the following year, intermarriage occurred in 10 of the 40 instances.[5]

The frequent appearance of Englishmen as jurors and especially as foremen of juries illustrates their growing numbers, active civic participation, and inevitable dominance in so many aspects of the community's life. The Dutch were by no means excluded, but the sheriffs, whom the English governor appointed and empowered to select jurors, were for several reasons more likely to choose Englishmen for service. Not only were the "twelve free and lawfull men" of the jury unknown to Dutch law, but English colonists were native speakers of the language used officially by the courts. Moreover, the law required that jurors be men of property with at least a £60 estate, which of course favored the English and French who formed a major percentage of Manhattan's wealthy males.[6] In the years from 1691 to 1710, jurymen on the Mayor's Court, which primarily handled civil cases, averaged 6.1 on the ten-internal scale used in this study to measure relative economic standing, while New Yorkers who did not serve scored only 4.8. Jurors on the Court of Quarter Sessions, which had some criminal jurisdiction, averaged 6.4, and foremen of this important court scored 8.6. As a result of these factors, English and French New Yorkers, although they composed only about 42 percent of the population, represented 52 percent of those in the

[5] *Coll. NYGBS*, IX, 70–95.

[6] "A Bill for Regulating and Returning of Able and Sufficient Jurors in the Tryalls at Law," May 16, 1699, *Col. Laws*, p. 388.

jury box, and English residents accounted for 18 of the 24 Quarter Sessions foremen.

Symbolically, the passage of the Ministry Act of 1693 and the erection of Trinity Church were the high points of the Fletcher years. The legislation, which affected New York, Queens, Richmond, and Westchester Counties, provided public support for a "good sufficient Protestant Minister to officiate and have the care of souls." [7] Despite opposition from Dissenters, the authorities interpreted the law to require the cleric to be ordained in the Church of England.

New York's Anglicans in November 1696 called William Vesey, a twenty-four year old native of Massachusetts, to be the city's "good sufficient Protestant Minister." A communicant of the Church of England since the age of fifteen, Vesey graduated from Harvard College in 1693. Too young to be ordained, he spent almost three years preaching in Long Island and Boston churches. After receiving the call from New York, Vesey went to England and gained an M.A. from Oxford. Ordained in August 1697, Vesey returned to Manhattan where he immediately allied himself with the Anti-Leislerians and officiated at the opening of the city's new Anglican church on March 13, 1698. [8]

Trinity Church was New York's most impressive building. The northwest corner of Smith and Wall Streets was the site originally chosen, but the founders apparently changed their minds and paid the city's small Lutheran congregation for a piece of land near Wall Street on the west side of Broadway,

[7] "An Act for Settling a Ministry and Raising a Maintenance for Them in the City of New York, County of Richmond, Westchester, and Queens County," Sept. 22, 1693, *ibid.*, pp. 328–29.

[8] Edwin T. Corwin and Hugh Hastings, eds., *Ecclesiastical Records of the State of New York* (Albany, 1901), II, 1175.

southwest of the public burial grounds. The Lutherans contributed another parcel behind this plot, which William Anderson of New Jersey had given them, and in return the Anglicans permitted them to bury their dead in the churchyard.[9]

Manhattan's foremost English residents took turns supervising the erection of their church. The former mayor William Merritt and the leading merchants Thomas Burroughs, Thomas Clarke, William Morris, and Ebenezer Willson were among those who served as overseers in the month of August 1697. Another prominent merchant and later a pirate, William Kidd, helped the project while in port by lending the runner and tackle from his ship for the raising of stones.[10]

Dr. Benjamin Bullivant, a knowledgeable traveler from Boston, described the church as being "of good brown square stone and brick exactly English fashion with a large square steeple at the west end." Trinity immediately became the house of worship for the province's English officials. Governor Fletcher had a canopied private pew built for his family in the eastern part of the church near the chancel, and at public expense had a gallery erected on the south side of the building for use by him and his council. Other English leaders in the community also obtained choice pews in the new house of worship.[11]

One year after the opening of Trinity Church, the Common Council appropriated £3000 to erect a new city hall. It was to replace the *Stadt Huys* built in the Dock Street area in 1643. The new edifice was located uptown at the northeast corner of Wall and Nassau Streets. The availability of open land perhaps dictated the choice of the site, but the construction of New York's second City Hall within one block of the recently com-

---

[9] Min. Ves., pp. 1–2.   [10] *Ibid.*, pp. 3, 14.

[11] Wayne Andrews, ed., "A Glance at New York in 1697: The Travel Diary of Dr. Benjamin Bullivant," *New-York Historical Society Quarterly,* XL (Jan. 1956), 62; Min. Ves.

pleted Anglican Church was a fitting symbol of the transformation of the city into an English community.[12]

Many Leislerians were not reconciled to the new order of the 1690s, but they had no choice but to keep silent. However, a major political change was occurring in England; the Whig Party was ascending to power. This naturally put into disfavor the Anti-Leislerian beneficiaries of New York's Tory colonial officials. By 1695 the Whigs controlled Parliament, and in May they granted the reversal of the bills of attainder against Jacob Leisler and Jacob Milborne which the rebel chieftain's son had long been seeking. Two years later the new ministry dismissed Governor Fletcher and commissioned an Irish peer, Richard Coote, the Earl of Bellomont, in his stead.[13]

Bellomont entered office in New York on April 2, 1698. His tenure began auspiciously as the predominantly Anti-Leislerian colonial assembly enacted "A Bill for the Reconcileing of Parties" which forbade citizens from harassing or up-braiding each other about their activities during the days of the rebellion. Unfortunately, the reconciliation did not occur, as Bellomont, an opponent of Fletcher while in England, soon found his allies in New York among the Leislerians. As a gesture of friendship, he authorized them in the fall of 1698 to exhume the bodies of Jacob Leisler and Jacob Milborne from their graves near the gallows and rebury the remains in the grounds of the Dutch church. The Earl named Leislerian leaders Abraham De Peyster, Samuel Staats, and Robert Walters to his Council, and removed from it their foes, including Nicholas Bayard, Gabriel Min-

---

[12] *Min. Com. Coun.*, Jan. 11, 1698, May 25 and Aug. 17, 1699, II, 68, 78, 81–82. This building later became Federal Hall, the first home of the U.S. Congress under the Constitution of 1787.

[13] "An Act for Reversing the Attainder of Jacob Leisler and Others," 1695, *DHNY*, II, 435–37; John D. Runcie, "The Problem of Anglo-American Politics in Bellomont's New York," *WMQ*, XXVI (Apr. 1969), 193–94; "Commission for the Earl of Bellomont," June 18, 1697, *DRNY*, IV, 266.

vielle, William Nicolls, and William Pinhorne. Bellomont commissioned Abraham De Peyster as colonel of the city's militia,
and appointed other Leislerians such as Martin Clock, Cornelius
and Johannes De Peyster, Isaac De Riemer, and David Provoost
to captaincies.[14]

Appalled by Fletcher's former activities, Bellomont set out to
repair the damage which his predecessor had done to the colony. Under "An Act for the Vacateing Breaking and Annulling
Several Extravagant Grants of Land . . . ," the new governor
repossessed the vast estates which the Anti-Leislerians acquired
from the government in the early 1690s. This legislation also
angered the Anglican leadership by returning to the governor's
use the King's Farm which Fletcher had leased to Trinity
Church. Bellomont argued that Fletcher had no authority to give
away lands reserved for the governors of the province, and he
belittled his predecessor's claims to have built Trinity Church.
The Earl noted that gifts given by members of all churches and
taxes collected through the Ministry Act, primarily from Dutch
and French citizens, made possible the construction.[15]

Bellomont irritated the merchants by his attacks on piracy and
smuggling. He accused Fletcher of befriending the most no-
torious buccaneers of the era, and claimed that even the customs
officials were co-operating with the smugglers.[16] The governor's efforts prompted the merchants to seek the assistance of
their correspondents and contacts in London, who advised the
Parliament that the "Earle by his Administration and illegall
proceedings has put such further hardships on the Merchants

[14] "A Bill for the Reconcileing of Parties," June 14, 1698, *Documents
Relating to Leisler,* pp. 394–97; "Order in Council on the Report of the Lords
of Trade of the 19th of October," Oct. 25, 1698, *DRNY,* IV, 411; "Army
List of the Province of New York, 1700," *DHNY,* I, 361–62.

[15] *Col. Laws,* pp. 412–17; "Reply of Mr. Weaver to Colonel Fletcher's
Answer," Jan. 9, 1698, *DRNY,* IV, 463.

[16] See Chapter 3.

and others the King's subjects there that without redress the Petitioners must be forced to withhold their trade thither.'' [17]

Contrary to these protestations, Bellomont actually fostered New York's commercial activities. Indeed, he worked vigorously to protect the privileges of New York City, especially against the attempts of New Jersey to establish a competitive free port at Perth Amboy. To emphasize his determination, in 1698 he seized the *Hester,* a ship owned in part by Governor Jeremiah Basse of New Jersey, as it prepared to sail from Perth Amboy to London without paying the New York duties. Local courts condemned the vessel and its cargo and sold the *Hester* for £315 to Bellomont's chief political ally, Abraham De Peyster.

The Court of King's Bench in England, taking jurisdiction in the case through use of a feigned issue, reversed the decision of the New York judges in 1700 and confirmed New Jersey's right to an independent port, but no crisis ensued. In 1702 New Jersey became a royal colony, and Perth Amboy, overshadowed by her powerful neighbor, slipped into obscurity. [18]

Fletcher's Anti-Leislerian adherents, motivated by factors beyond a simple lust for land and illicit trade, paid little attention to Bellomont's efforts on behalf of New York City. The earl's enemies denounced him for filling the assembly and the militia with indigent Dutch, and William Vesey, Trinity's pastor, protested to Archbishop Tenison in England that ''our Governor has used all methods to destroy us and support dissenters.'' Nicholas Bayard succinctly expressed the feelings of the Anti-Leislerian faction with his complaint that ''most of the meanest and those of Dutch extractions have been put in all the

[17] ''Petition of London Merchants Trading to New York,'' Feb. 14, 1700, *DRNY,* IV, 604–5.
[18] Charles McLean Andrews, *The Colonial Period of American History* (New Haven, 1937), III, 180n.

offices and places of trust and power; by which means most of the principal and peaceable inhabitants and especially those of the English nation have been opprest.'' [19]

Bellomont and his Leislerian allies agreed with their opponents' recognition of the role of ethnic background in the New York struggle. The new governor complained to the Lords of Trade that Fletcher had ''supported a few rascally English who are a scandall to their nation and the Protestant Religion . . . and severely used the Dutch, except some few Merchants, whose trade he favored, who ought to have an equal benefit of the English Governt who are most hearty for his present Mjty and are a sober industrious people and obedient to Governt.'' Bellomont further condemned the clique which surrounded his predecessor for aggravating the situation by appropriating the sobriquet, the ''English party.'' The anonymous Leislerian author of the tract ''Loyalty Vindicated . . .'' also attacked that group for rekindling the animosities between ''those of a *Dutch* extraction (who are the most numerous, Loyal and Sober Subjects of that Province) and the few *English* (who were most averse and backward in the Revolution, but violent and bloody in the Execution of Capt. *Leisler,* as well as the most dissolute in their Morals) in this Province. . . .'' [20]

As passions flared, the rapport of the early 1690s faded. Mar-

[19] ''Earl of Bellomont to the Lords of the Treasury,'' May 25, 1698; ''Heads of Accusation against the Earl of Bellomont,'' Mar. 11, 1700; ''Colonel Nicholas Bayard to Sir Philip Meadows,'' Mar. 8, 1701, *DRNY,* IV, 317–18, 620–23, 848; Runcie, ''Anglo-American Politics,'' pp. 205–6, 210.

[20] ''Earl of Bellomont to the Lords of Trade,'' June 22, 1698; ''Earl of Bellomont to the Lords of the Treasury,'' May 25, 1698, *DRNY,* IV, 325–26, 317; ''Loyalty Vindicated, Being an Answer to a Late False, Seditious, and Scandalous Pamphlet, Entitled, 'A Letter from a Gent., Etc.' [''A Letter from a Gentleman of New York concerning the Troubles Which Happened in That Province, in the Time of the Late Happy Revolution''] Published for the Sake of Truth and Justice, by a Hearty Lover of King William and the Protestant Religion,'' Oct. 28, 1698, *Documents Relating to Leisler,* p. 388.

riages between Dutch and English inhabitants again became rare in the Reformed Church, occurring in only 8 of the 196 weddings from 1698 through 1701. Leislerian candidates reappeared and made successful challenges for aldermanic posts. In one of the more outstanding cases, Nicholas Roosevelt in 1700 replaced Brandt Schuyler, who had served as alderman for the South Ward eight times in the 1690s.[21]

New York's population had divided into two political groups which soon exhibited a degree of organization and voter allegiance characteristic of more modern parties. The opposing sides presented full slates of candidates and the citizenry responded by voting for unified tickets. In the provincial election of 1698, New York City residents authorized to send four men to the assembly announced their preference for only one candidate with the understanding that they also wanted the three other contestants who were associated with him. Governor Bellomont explained that "the freemen or electors on both sides did by a tacit consent name one candidate only, expressing the rest by the word (Company) and this they did, it seems, to save time because there were four candidates of a side, whom it would have been tedious to name. As for example, the Leisler party voted for the Mayor of New Yorke and Company; the others (whom the Leislerites call the Jacobite party) voted for Mr. Wenham and Company."[22]

Bellomont's sudden death on March 5, 1701, only worsened the conflict. His youthful nephew, Lieutenant Governor John Nanfan, succeeded him but was not a strong figure. Nanfan did not immediately align himself with any faction, and his failure clearly to grant the favor of the royal executive to either group created a very unstable situation. During Nanfan's tenure as in-

[21] *Coll. NYGBS*, IX, 87–96; *Min. Com. Coun.*, Sept. 29, 1700, II, 116.

[22] "Earl of Bellomont to the Lords of Trade," Apr. 27, 1699, *DRNY*, IV, 508.

terim executive the Leislerians and the Anti-Leislerians fought bitterly for control of the city and colony. On the municipal level, the struggle culminated in the disputed election of 1701, which again laid bare the role of national backgrounds in the city's politics.

As the Dongan Charter required, Manhattan's Common Council election took place on September 29, the feast of St. Michael the Archangel. The contests for the posts of alderman and assistant in the East, West, and South Wards were especially heated. In the East Ward a member of one of the city's most distinguished Dutch mercantile families, the Leislerian Johannes De Peyster, whom Bellomont appointed mayor in September 1698, opposed the Anti-Leislerian English merchant William Morris for alderman; the Leislerian Abraham Brazier, a Dutch pumpmaker, stood against the Anti-Leislerian English merchant Jeremiah Tothill for assistant. In the West Ward the Dutch coopers Johannes De Provoost and Peter Willemse Roome, both Leislerians, vied with two Anti-Leislerian Englishmen, John Hutchins, a gentleman who was a large landowner in the newer area of the district, and Robert White, a carpenter, for seats as alderman and assistant respectively. In the South Ward the Leislerian Nicholas Roosevelt, a bolter, ran against another Dutchman, the Anti-Leislerian merchant Brandt Schuyler, for alderman, and two more Dutch citizens, the Leislerian Hendrick Jelleson, a cordwainer, and the Anti-Leislerian Johannes Johnson, were candidates for assistant.[23]

[23] Waldron Phoenix Belknap, Jr., *The De Peyster Genealogy* (Boston, 1956), pp. 14–16; Con. Lib., Sept. 10, 1692, XVIII, 181–85; Aug. 20, 1695; Nov. 27, 1695, XXI, 71–74, 104–5; May 9, 1696, XXIII, 234–36; *The Burghers of New Amsterdam and the Freemen of New York, 1675–1866,* in the *Coll. NYHS,* XVIII (1885), p. 62; Min. Ves., p. 24; Andrew J. Provost, *Biographical and Genealogical Notes of the Provost Family from 1545 to 1831* (New York, 1952); Peter Roome Warner, *Descendants of Peter Willemse Roome* (New York, 1883), p. 5; Charles Barney Whittelsey, *The Roosevelt*

On the morning of October 14, 1701, the day set by the charter for new officeholders to assume their posts, Thomas Noell, an English merchant, took the oath as mayor of New York. After attending services at Trinity Church, Noell proceeded to the courthouse where he received the city's charter and seal from his predecessor the Dutch Leislerian merchant, Isaac De Riemer. Noell then told his clerk to swear in the members of the Common Council elected on September 29, but only the English merchants Philip French and Robert Lurting, the Anti-Leislerians chosen as aldermen and assistant in the Dock Ward, stepped forward. The Leislerian candidates who claimed victory in the East, West, and South Wards asserted that they had already taken the oath from the outgoing mayor. At the same time, the Anti-Leislerian candidates from the same wards disputed the election returns, presented Noell with writs of mandamus, and demanded to be declared the rightful winners. The newly elected alderman and assistant from the North Ward, the Dutch Leislerians Jacob Boelen and Gerrett Onclebagh, both of whom were goldsmiths, also declined to take the oath from Noell, but no one challenged their claim to victory.[24]

In order to prevent disorders, Noell adjourned the proceedings so that he could examine the records for precedents. He correctly determined that the incoming rather than the outgoing mayor properly swore in the new municipal officers, and he consequently ordered an examination of the elections in the disputed districts. He appointed three boards of four investigators each, and included two members of each faction on all three boards. In the East Ward, Noell named two merchants,

---

Genealogy, 1649–1902 (Hartford, Conn., 1902), p. 7; *Abstracts of Wills,* in the *Coll. NYHS,* XXVI (1893), 430; for Hutchins's landholding activities see Chapter 4.

[24] *Min. Com. Coun.,* Nov. 11, 1701, II, 159–60; Con. Lib., May 14, 1694; May 6, 1696, XXI, 97–98, 102–3.

Lawrence Reade, an Englishman, and Benjamin Faneuil, a
Frenchman, for the Anti-Leislerians, and two Dutchmen, Barent
Reynders, a sailmaker, and Johannes Hardenbrooke, a merchant, for the Leislerians. In the West Ward, the French merchant John Barbarie and the Dutch mason Dirck Vanderburgh, a
communicant of Trinity Church, represented the Anti-
Leislerians, and two Dutch residents, Jacob Goelet, a brick-
maker, and Issac Sloover, a shopkeeper, the Leislerian interests.
In the South Ward, Noell appointed two merchants, the Englishman Matthew Ling and the extraordinarily successful Dutchman
Rip Van Dam, on behalf of the Anti-Leislerians; the mayor
selected two Dutch citizens, Johannes Van Giesen, a carpenter,
and Gysbert Vaninburgh, a baker, to serve for the Leislerians.[25]

The Leislerians, believing that the Englishman Noell would
not be impartial, or perhaps fearing that their successes would
not bear scrutiny, refused to participate in the examination of
the polls. The Anti-Leislerians then had no such hesitance and
naturally declared their candidates to be the victors. The Supreme Court of the province imposed the final solution, which
bore the signs of compromise. The judges named the Leislerians
De Peyster and Brazier to be alderman and assistant in the East
Ward; the Anti-Leislerian pairs, Hutchins and White, and
Schuyler and Johnson, to assume the posts in the West and
South Wards respectively. The original Anti-Leislerian winners
on the Dock Ward and the Leislerian victors in the North Ward
retained their seats.[26]

[25] Con. Lib., May 13, 1686, XIII, 225–26; Feb. 18, 1701, XXV, 32–35;
Dec. 16, 1710, XXVI, 451–53; Min. Ves., p. 46; Mrs. John A. Weisse,
A History of the Bethune Family Together with a Sketch of the Faneuil Family
(New York, 1884), p. 45; *Burghers and Freemen,* pp. 59, 65–66, 71; for Van
Dam's activities, see Chapter 3.

[26] *Min. Com. Coun.,* Nov. 11, 1701, II, 161–63, 165–68, 170, 172–73,
176; Paul M. Hamlin and Charles E. Baker, *Supreme Court of Judicature of
the Province of New York, 1691–1704* (New York, 1959), II, 341–44.

If nothing else, this controversy produced unusual information about New York's political life. As part of their review procedures, the arbiters appointed by Mayor Noell examined the polls made by canvassing officials in the East, West, and South Wards. These records noted the persons who ran for the offices of alderman and assistant in each disputed district, and listed by name the citizens who voted for each candidate. Published by the Common Council as evidence, the election returns provide not only information about the divisions within the city's leadership, but are also an untapped source of data on the bases of popular support enjoyed by the contending factions.[27]

Participation in the election was at a high level. Of the 500 adult males in the East, West, and South Wards who have been included in the group of 876 New Yorkers under study, 262 voted in the 1701 election. Since some of the nonvoters must have been minors, perhaps as much as 60 percent of the potential electorate cast ballots.

Apparently, a relatively broad franchise made possible large-scale popular involvement in the political process. Of the 262 persons who participated, 48 or 18 percent ranked in the lowest bracket of the five-interval scale of wealth, a strong indication that economic restrictions on the exercise of the franchise were virtually nonexistent. Not even tenancy was a cause for disfranchisement. Indeed, only women, indentured servants, minors, persons going to the polls outside their home district, and inhabitants who were not taxable had their ballots discarded. These last were probably transients because the law made all persons liable for taxes after just one month's residence.[28]

[27] *Min. Com. Coun,* Nov. 11, 1701, II, 163–79.

[28] *Ibid.,* p. 163; "An Act to Enable the City of New York to Relieve the Poor and Defray Their Necesary and Public Charge," July 3, 1695, *Col. Laws,* p. 350; David T. Valentine, *History of the City of New York* (New York, 1853), pp. 251–52.

Although New York's less affluent had the franchise, the well-to-do were more likely to vote. Whereas 42 percent of the persons in the lowest bracket on the five-interval scale of wealth cast ballots, 49, 53, 52, and 71 percent of the citizens in the second, middle, fourth, and highest brackets, respectively, went to the polls. The greater stake of the affluent in governmental action and their better access to information about public affairs produced a process of social selection by which the wealthy comprised a disproportionately large portion of the actual voters.

The municipal elections showed not only that two factions existed but that the public responded to their appeals for support. As in the colonial assembly election described by Bellomont, the citizens who participated in the Common Council contest of 1701 were divided into Leislerians and Anti-Leislerians. The returns demonstrate that persons who voted for the aldermanic aspirant of one faction invariably also cast ballots for his associate seeking the office of assistant. And the wording of a presentment made by the grand jury accusing De Peyster, Provoost, and Roosevelt of "returning themselves as aldermen of the City of New York and other persons assistants, assessors, collectors, and constables" implies that the parties may have presented single slates of candidates for all elected municipal offices.[29]

Dutch residents gave overwhelming loyalty to the Leislerian candidates; 132 of the 262 voting males were definitely identified as Hollanders, and 112 of them or 85 percent cast their ballots for De Peyster, Provoost, or Roosevelt. The Leislerians won without dispute in the North Ward, where the Dutch comprised 78 percent of the population, and lost decisively in the Dock Ward, the only district where the English and French formed a majority. Englishmen and Frenchmen were almost

[29] *Min. Com. Coun.*, Nov. 11, 1701, II, 163–76; Hamlin and Baker, *Supreme Court*, I, 153n.

unanimously Anti-Leislerian; 60 out of 66 of the former, and 40 out of 41 of the latter chose Morris, Hutchins, or Schuyler.

Inclusion in these figures of voters whose ethnic backgrounds have been only tentatively identified confirms the results. Of 138 persons categorized as Dutch, 113 or 83 percent voted for the Leislerians. Of 77 citizens classed as English, 69 voted for the Anti-Leislerians. Of 43 residents categorized as French, 42 voted for the Anti-Leislerians.

Analysis of the data on ethnic background, economic standing, commercial activity, and occupational pursuit available for 213 of the 262 voters further indicates that national background was the most important factor distinguishing the Leislerians from the Anti-Leislerians. By using a multiple regression test we can measure the relative importance of various social and economic characteristics in determining social behavior. Ethnic background produced a high partial correlation coefficient of 0.69542, and after all the other factors accounted for as much of the phenomenon as they could, it independently accounted for an extraordinarily high 53.8 percent of the variation. Used as a descriptive statistic, the "T" value of 13.78812 generated by the ethnic variable suggests that such a pattern of relationship could occur accidentally far less than .001 percent of the time (Table 10).

The cross-tabulation test is another form of statistical analysis. Though less advanced than regression analysis, it is more familiar in historical research. It also tests the strength of the relationships between dependent variables and a phenomenon under investigation, but it measures the impact of each variable independently without controlling for the effect of the other factors under consideration. This study used cross-tabulation as a supplement to the regression analysis.[30]

---

[30] See discussion of these procedures in the Essay on Sources and Methods.

Due to the limited number of variables the program employed could handle, the sample of voters was restricted to 185 persons. This included all those who participated in occupations in which at least 4 others in the test population of 876 were involved. The test took into account voting behavior, ethnic background, economic rank, occupation, and level of commercial activity.

Table 10. Results of a multiple regression test of the factors affecting political affiliation in the elections of 1701

Variables	Partial correlation coefficient	T. value	Proportion of cumulative variation (in %)
Ethnic background	−0.69542	−13.78812	53.8
Date of marriage	0.00442	0.06300	00.0
Employment & social position			
Skilled & unskilled trades	0.19843	2.88453	00.6
Services	0.13279	1.91144	00.0
Food production & distribution	0.15558	2.44030	00.1
Seafaring trades	0.18511	2.68384	00.3
Merchants & gentlemen	0.16898	2.44279	01.3
Economic standing	0.04798	0.68447	00.0
Relative mercantile importance	−0.11793	−1.69211	00.6
Total variation explained: 56%			

Source: W. J. Dixon, ed., *BMD—Biomedical Computer Programs* (Los Angeles, 1967); and others cited previously

Cross-tabulation analysis confirms the primacy of ethnic background as a determinant of party affiliation. In separate tests, Dutch nationality combined with Leislerian support to produce a correlation coefficient of 0.71, and English and French background combined with Anti-Leislerianism to produce one of 0.69. No other variable generated a coefficient higher than 0.28.

These statistics confirm the evaluation reported to the Lords of Trade by the provincial attorney general, Sampson Shelton Broughton, shortly before the 1701 election. ''I finde two very opposite parties amongst this people,'' wrote Broughton, ''all equally the King's subjects, yet want to be distinguished for nation sake. And I cannot discern a more material ground of their difference than that; tho many allegations are on both sides." [31]

As Table 10 indicates, wealth did not significantly affect political affiliation. According to the ten-interval scale of wealth the typical Leislerian among the 262 voters scored an average of 5.35, just slightly more than the 5.31 tallied by his Anti-Leislerian counterpart. When compared in terms of the five-interval scale, the two factions were well represented in every category. In the top and bottom brackets, in which the English and French were proportionately overrepresented, the Anti-Leislerians won 60 and 58 percent of the votes respectively. They won 47, 52, and 52 percent in the second lowest, middle, and second highest intervals, respectively.

Occupational background also bore little apparent relation to political preference. Only 10 merchants voted for Leislerian candidates, while 30 cast their ballots for the opposition, but even in this instance the breakdown followed ethnic more than professional lines. Of the 10 Leislerian merchants, 8 were Dutch, and of the 29 Anti-Leislerian traders whose nationalities are known, 24 were English or French. The political preferences of the cordwainers similarly show the ethnic basis of New York City's politics. Of the 16 cordwainers who cast ballots, 15 were Leislerians and only one was an Anti-Leislerian; but all of the former were Dutch and the latter was an Englishman.

Age did bear a subtle relation to political affiliation. Judging from data obtained about 107 of the voters, Leislerian candidates drew their strongest support from Dutch New Yorkers who married between 1686 and 1695. Born around the time of the English conquest, these persons represented the first generation to feel its full impact on the province's social structure.

[31] "Attorney General Broughton to the Lords of Trade," Sept. 3, 1701, *DRNY*, IV, 914.

Aliens in their homeland, they found Leisler's movement an especially attractive opportunity and a call to assert themselves. Out of 24, 23 voted for De Peyster, Provoost, or Roosevelt. Leislerism exerted a powerful but more modest influence on the older and younger members of the Dutch community. Of the 20 who took spouses between 1676 and 1685, 15 cast their ballots for the faction's candidates in 1701, while 25 of the 33 wed after 1695 did the same.

Englishmen and Huguenots, regardless of age, uniformly opposed the Leislerians. Neither group could find any relevance in a movement of displaced Dutchmen, and the English were able to identify with their countrymen among the Anti-Leislerian leadership. Of the 40 voters in the English and French community for whom marriage dates are available, 35 cast their ballots for Morris, Hutchins, or Schuyler.

Spawned as a protest by a majority of Dutch descendants of New Amsterdam against the growing influence of the English, French, and a few cooperative Dutch grandees in New York, the Leislerian agitation inevitably grew weaker as time passed. The composite voter–marriage date statistics succinctly delineate the history of the period. The Leislerians won the allegiance of 18 of the 23 voters known to have married between 1676 and 1686, when the Dutch composed the vast majority of the population. Although they captured 96 percent of the Dutch who took spouses between 1686 and 1695, the period when English and French dominance became clear, the Leislerians won the support of only 23 of the total of 38 voters who were married in those years. Finally, the Leislerians became a minority among the youngest voters, winning the allegiance of only 27 of the 56 voters who were wed after 1695, when the English and French formed a large minority of the inhabitants.

After the election of 1701, the Leislerians, to whom Nanfan finally gave his support, managed temporarily to maintain control of the colony and to make their enemies uncomfortable. In

April 1702 they outlawed the English merchants Philip French and Thomas Wenham who had fled the province to avoid prosecution for circulating petitions against the government.[32] In February of the same year they attempted to avenge the death of Jacob Leisler by accusing his nemesis, Nicholas Bayard, of treason for having sought signatures on petitions against the government. The Leislerian solicitor general Thomas Weaver attended the sessions of the grand jury which indicted Bayard and controlled their access to witnesses. Of course, Weaver's actions may not have been necessary since several grand jurors allegedly stated before considering the evidence "that if Bayard's neck were made of gold he should be hanged." After a parody of a trial, the jurors, all of whom allegedly were Dutch and many of whom were illiterate in the English language, found the defendant guilty, and the court condemned him to death. Only a reprieve from England saved Bayard from Leisler's fate on the gallows.[33]

Material gains supplemented the psychological satisfactions of revenge which the Leislerians enjoyed during Nanfan's tenure. The supporters of the administration did not manage to repeat the land grab accomplished by the Anti-Leislerians under Fletcher, but they did request and receive substantial grants of acreage. The names of Jacob Leisler's widowed daughter Susannah Vaughton and his son-in-law Robert Walters appear several times in the land records for these years, as do those of several of the rebel's supporters, including Samuel Staats and David Provoost.[34]

The arrival of Edward Hyde, Lord Cornbury, in New York in

[32] "An Act for Outlawing Philip French and Thomas Wenham Merchants and Enforcing Process of Outlawry," Apr. 30, 1702, *Col. Laws,* pp. 476–77.

[33] "Bayard Trial," John D. Lawson, ed., *American State Trials* (St. Louis, 1918), X, 522–25.

[34] Secretary of State, New York State, *Calendar of New York Colonial Manuscripts: Indorsed Land Papers in the Office of the Secretary of State of New York, 1643–1803* (Albany, 1864), pp. 56–59.

May 1702 marked the end of John Nanfan's interim rule. The Lords of Trade followed Sampson Shelton Broughton's advice to instruct the new appointee "to use temper and moderation at his first coming to us, and to treat each party with like favour and respect," but Cornbury, a Tory, restored to power the Anti-Leislerians who had opposed his Whig predecessor. Tenures in office again increased as political stability returned to the colony. The English merchants William Peartree and Ebenezer Willson each served three consecutive terms as mayor between 1703 and 1710. Aldermen also held their posts for longer times. The Leislerians managed to maintain control of the North Ward, where David Provoost won seven elections, but the Anti-Leislerians fared better in other districts. In the West Ward, for example, the Anti-Leislerians Dirck Vanderburgh and William Smith served, respectively, three and four terms.[35]

By the time Robert Hunter replaced Cornbury as governor in 1710, the strength of the Leislerian movement had dissipated. The steady increase in the number of English and French residents in the population and the aging or death of persons who remembered the Dutch days precluded further attempts to restore the old order. During Hunter's administration, disputes over the power of the colonial assembly marked the beginning of a new period of politics.

Hunter's tenure in office, which lasted until 1719, was a period of at least partial reunification of the city's contending groups. Politically, the governor integrated both factions on his council. The Leislerians Abraham De Peyster, Samuel Staats, and Robert Walters took seats, as did the Anti-Leislerians John Barbarie, Caleb Heathcote, and Rip Van Dam.[36] Socially and

---

[35] "Broughton to the Lords of Trade," p. 914; *Min. Com. Coun.*, Sept. 29, 1702–1710; Oct. 11, 1705; Oct. 1 and 14, 1706; II, 202, 239–40, 271–72, 286–88, 308–10, 329, 361–62, 383–84, 416.

[36] Jerome Reich, *Leisler's Rebellion: A Study of Democracy in New York, 1664–1720* (Chicago, 1953), pp. 167–68.

symbolically, the white fear of black conspiracy and the violent reaction to the slave uprising of 1712 re-emphasized a fundamental similarity of interests among European colonists of all national backgrounds.

In the early years of the eighteenth century New Yorkers became unusually concerned about the dangers posed by their bondsmen. The murder of a Queens County family in 1708 led to the execution of four Negroes with "all the torment possible for a terror to others," and to the enactment of "An Act for Preventing the Conspiracy of Slaves." In the same period the courts heard a large number of cases concerning individuals accused of illegally entertaining slaves in their homes or ale houses.[37]

April 1712 brought to a climax the festering relations of white New Yorkers and their bondsmen. In the early hours of April 6, a group of slaves set fire to a house in the East Ward and then murdered 9 whites and wounded 12 others who came to help put out the blaze. Within two weeks, the courts indicted 43 Negroes and Indians of murder or attempted murder, convicted 25, and summarily executed 18. The ghastliness of some of the executions, including the eight-to-ten hour roasting of Nicholas Roosevelt's slave Tom, indicates the hysterical quality of the community's desire for revenge.[38]

Black bondsmen were a suitable scapegoat to unify New York's white population. The Africans, whose numbers multiplied rapidly early in the eighteenth century, served as a common enemy for the Dutch, English, and French who held them in servitude.[39] Fresher fears of a racially different, subversive

[37] *Col. Laws,* Oct. 30, 1708, p. 631; see, for example, New York City, Minutes of the Court of Quarter Sessions, pp. 112–13, 186–87, 188–89.

[38] Kenneth Scott, "The Slave Insurrection in New York in 1712," *New-York Historical Society Quarterly,* XLV (Jan. 1961), 43–74.

[39] Edgar J. McManus, *A History of Negro Slavery in New York* (Syracuse, N.Y., 1966), pp. 23, 24, 26.

element in the population submerged the remnants of outdated hostilities bred by national competition for dominance in Manhattan, and brought an end to the first episode in the politics of ethnicity in New York City.

7 ∽ Conclusion

New York City, and by extension New York Colony, of which it was the economic, political, and population center, exhibited attributes common to most colonial settlements. By the end of the seventeenth century, clear lines of economic stratification had appeared, and well-to-do citizens controlled a major share of the community's wealth. Political life manifested the deferential character typical of the era. The wealthy held office, and the richest men held the highest posts. Secure in their status, they encouraged broad but passive citizen participation in civic matters, and residents had ready access to the vote.

Like Virginia, Massachusetts, and Maryland, New York experienced in the latter years of the seventeenth century a crisis of maturation. Although the circumstances in each case were unique, in all four provinces the trouble had its roots in a division within the elite. The ensuing struggles had important effects on the structure of each colony's society and set the stage for the emergence of new political issues in the eighteenth century.

Beneath the superficialities, however, New York's politics had extraordinary qualities generated by the ethnic heterogeneity of the population, which was New York's most distinguishing characteristic. The existence of cleavages between the descendants of the Dutch founders and the later English and French arrivals, which ran parallel to divisions between the older, declining elite and the newer, aspiring one, divided the community into two opposing camps, identifiable on the basis of national backgrounds, and created strong emotional bonds between followers and leaders in each. This undermined the politics of deference and gave the people an initial encounter with democratically-oriented politics.

The distribution of wealth in New York City resembled that in Boston, the other long established city of the northern colonies. In New York in 1703 the richest 10 percent of the taxpayers owned 47 percent of the assessed resources; in Boston in 1687 the comparable group controlled about 42 percent.[1]

New York also resembled the other American cities and colonies in the concentration of political power in the hands of the wealthy.[2] New Yorkers, regardless of what faction they belonged to, gave their allegiance to the well-to-do. Abraham De Peyster, an eminent Leislerian spokesman during the administration of Governor Bellomont, and Nicholas Bayard, his counterpart in the opposing camp, were among the five richest men in the city. And evidence for New York shows that, as in Boston, the holders of major offices were more affluent than the men in lesser posts. On the ten-interval scale used in this study to measure relative economic standing, the city's assemblymen averaged 9.4, aldermen 9.3, assistants 8.2, assessors 7.9, and constables 7.0. Even collectors, the elected officials with the least average wealth, registered 6.7, more than two full units above the mean score of 4.5 for nonofficeholders.

Relatively few men held public office, though the size of the population was small compared to the number of posts to be filled annually. Of the 738 male heads of family examined in

[1] See Chapter 2; also James A. Henretta, "Economic Development and Social Structure in Colonial Boston," *WMQ*, XXII (Jan. 1965), 75–92.

[2] For discussions of this phenomenon, see Leonard W. Labaree, *Conservatism in Early American History* (New York, 1948), and Charles S. Sydnor, *American Revolutionaries in the Making* (New York, 1965).

this study, 197 or 26 percent held an elective or appointive position at some time during the twenty years from 1691 through 1710. Most of them held minor assignments as assessors, collectors, or constables, and had no vote on the Common Council. Only 74 men, or 10 percent of the males included in the study, sat as assistants or in a higher capacity. A mere 48 or 6.5 percent managed to attain the municipal posts of mayor, recorder, or aldermen, with their legislative and judicial powers, or served in the provincial hierarchy as lieutenant governor, member of the Governor's Council, assemblyman, or judge.

Ranking New York's 197 public officials on a ten-interval scale of political influence, derived from a matrix which assigned values according to the importance of the posts held and the lengths of tenure, illustrates even more dramatically the narrow concentration of power in the city. The matrix is biased to present as conservative a view as possible, but the politicians who formed the upper tenth of the group still made a strikingly high score.[3] These 20 New Yorkers accounted for 892 points or 52 percent of the total of 1723 points generated by the matrix. In these terms less than 3 percent of the city's male population exercised half of the official civic power (Figure 2).

Retention of so much power by so few individuals is not surprising. Practicality demanded that moneyed men hold office, for they were the only persons with the means and education to execute the obligation effectively. City officials received no pay, and despite the lucrative fees available in some posts, the loss of time from business activities and the social expenses involved probably made politics a costly endeavor. Leonard Lewis, who ranked in the ninth bracket of the ten-interval scale of economic standing, declined to accept re-election as alderman for the East Ward in 1699 because he had already served

[3] See Essay on Sources and Methods for discussion of the matrix.

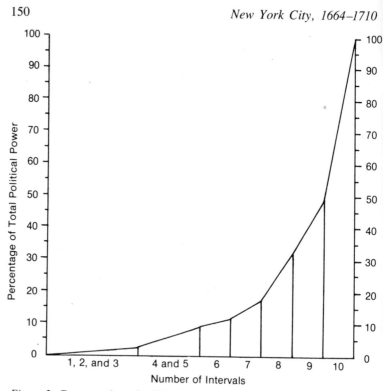

Figure 2. Concentration of political power

three terms and the duty interfered with his business activities.[4]
How then could less affluent citizens afford to neglect their
employments to serve the public?

Belief and convention sanctioned what necessity dictated. In
the days of Dutch rule, the inhabitants were instructed by the
council to nominate only the wealthiest burghers for office.[5] Ordinary citizens thought it natural to depend on the elite for guidance on matters of common concern. In an age when the idea of

---

[4] *Min. Com. Coun.*, Oct. 16, 1699, II, 92.

[5] "Minutes of Council of New Netherland, 1673, 1674," Aug. 16 and 17,
1673, *DRNY*, II, 574–75.

man's inequality was a truism, custom and public opinion associated the attributes of virtue and talent expected of leaders with the possession of property and high family status.

Citizens of New York, like those of other colonies, enjoyed a broadly available franchise. Entrenched in power, the elite had no objections to liberal voting arrangements. Indeed, in New York, they led the call for the ballot. Mayor Cornelius Steenwyck, Deputy Mayor William Beeckman, and Aldermen Johannes Van Brugh, John Lawrence, Pieter Jacobs Marius, James Graham, and Nicholas Bayard signed the petition of November 9, 1683 to Governor Thomas Dongan which requested the election of local officials.[6] They were asking for a standard municipal privilege and evidently saw in it no threat to their security, and indeed may have desired the ballot as a means of reinforcing their claims to local autonomy against the encroachment of higher authorities. In any potential contest prominent natives would be likely to defeat the candidates of any outside agency.

A broad franchise was also a means of social control. Colonial governments lacked substantive institutional means of coercion, and the elected officers at times found themselves personally responsible for maintaining the peace.[7] The leadership could not rule without evident popular support, and voting had the major function of providing the needed constitutional and symbolic affirmation of their authority. Consequently the gov-

[6] "Petition of the Mayor and Common Council of New York for a New Charter," Nov. 9, 1683, *ibid.*, III, 337–39.

[7] In August 1696, for example, Mayor William Merritt personally confronted a number of slaves who were creating a disturbance near his home. One of them struck Merritt in the face, and the following day the mayor reported the incident to the other justices of the peace, who had the offender punished. New York City, Minutes of the Court of Quarter Sessions, Aug. 28, 1696, Criminal Court Building, New York, pp. 15–16.

ernment tried to extend the franchise as much as possible. In 1695, after the return of political calm, the city expanded its electoral base by reducing the fee for purchasing a freemanship, which authorized its holder to carry on his business and to vote. In a move perhaps calculated to appeal to the Dutch who formed a large majority of the long-time residents, the new fee was set at ninepence (9d.) for persons living in the city since 1686. But many New Yorkers were reluctant to pay even this modest charge, and the government did not attempt to preserve a monopoly of economic or political privileges for freemen. The records state that the city's "inhabitants" constituted the electorate, and indeed, it seems that, at least in municipal elections, any taxpaying resident could vote.[8]

Voting in the seventeenth and eighteenth centuries, however, was not designed to promote competition for control of the government. Efforts by political groups to activate broad-based electoral support would have vitiated the franchise as a stabilizing force. New Yorkers did not consider factionalism and political strife desirable or necessary. The occasional rejection of office by the voters' designee suggests that elections were frequently uncontested and that heated races were unusual. When disputed elections did occur they created obvious cracks in the foundation of popular affirmation, and usually produced legislation to reinforce the structure. After the bitter controversies surrounding the 1701 contests in New York City, the assembly enacted a measure clarifying the municipal election procedures in order to preserve "the peace, Welfare, and quiet of the Inhabitants Freeholders and Freemen" and to insure that "all heats Animosities Quarrels Strifes & Debates may for the

[8] Beverly McAnear, "The Place of the Freeman in Old New York," *New York History,* XXI (Oct. 1940), 420; *Min. Com. Coun.,* Nov. 11, 1701, II, 163.

future be laid aside & those already happened for ever hereafter be buried in Oblivion.'' [9]

Deference and a broad franchise could coexist in most colonies because the nature of politics produced a passive electorate. The purpose of government was largely administration of the status quo rather than the enactment of legislation, and accordingly, officials did not propose far-reaching social programs which might excite the voters. Nor was the elite which provided leadership about to threaten its privileged position by encouraging antagonism between the common people and the wealthy. Of course, legislatures passed measures favoring special groups like merchants and planters, and the members of the elite often fought each other viciously for power and its spoils.

Nathaniel Bacon of Virginia and his associates, for example, represented a group of substantial planters. Many of them were recent arrivals in the province who found their access to power and privilege blocked by the clique established around the long-time governor, William Berkeley. The merchants who overthrew Governor Andros in Massachusetts had gained wealth but not a commensurate amount of economic power in the decades after the founding of the colony. They had aided Edward Randolph's successful efforts to have the charter of the Puritan government annulled, but they still found themselves in a subordinate position under the Dominion of New England. The men of Maryland's Association Convention, which provided the leadership backbone of John Coode's Rebellion of 1689, were Protestants who had come to the colony in the decades after 1659. The sons of well-to-do Englishmen, they prospered in America and gained local prominence, but found the path to

[9] ''An Act for Declareing Confirming and Explaining the Libertys of the City of New York Relating to Ye Election of Their Magistrats,'' May 1, 1702, *Col. Laws,* p. 490.

greater success blocked by the retainers of Lord Baltimore, many of whom were Catholics.[10]

At crucial moments in these struggles, though, some politicians turned to the citizenry for support. Bacon found a warm reception among the Virginia frontiersmen, whose problems with the Indians he deftly blamed on Governor Berkeley. Confronted with a new common menace, the Massachusetts merchants joined forces with their old Puritan foes to arouse the Bay Colony settlers against the Anglicanism of Governor Andros. And Coode played upon the terror of Catholicism common among seventeenth century Protestants in galvanizing opposition to Lord Baltimore.[11]

Such appeals to the public were usually short-lived, however, and the divisions which they generated among the citizens did not persist. Once Bacon had failed and the victorious elite ceased its purges, factional identities disappeared and no stable political alignments developed. The Glorious Revolution did not divide the people of Massachusetts, and except for the witchcraft trials at Salem, the province quickly regained calm. In Maryland, the victorious Protestants inhibited the development of a permanent opposition by imposing political liabilities on the Catholics in the population.[12]

New York was the major exception to this pattern. There, the conquest of 1664, not the Glorious Revolution, marked the turn-

[10] Bernard Bailyn, "Politics and Social Structure in Virginia," in James M. Smith, ed., *Seventeenth-Century America* (Chapel Hill, N.C., 1959), pp. 90–115; Bernard Bailyn, *The New England Merchants in the Seventeenth Century* (Cambridge, Mass., 1955), pp. 168–70; Lois Green Carr and David William Jordan, *Maryland's Revolution of Government, 1689–1692* (Ithaca, N.Y., 1974), pp. 65–72, 221.

[11] Bailyn, "Politics and Social Structure;" Bailyn, *New England Merchants;* Carr and Jordan, *Maryland's Revolution.*

[12] Bailyn, "Politics and Social Structure;" Chadwick Hansen, *Witchcraft at Salem* (New York, 1969), ch. 8; Carr and Jordan, *Maryland's Revolution,* p. 218.

ing point of seventeenth century history. In the aftermath of the take-over, numbers of Englishmen and Huguenots came to the province, and although still a minority at the end of the century, they had seized effective control of the city. Some Dutch remained competitive and fared well under English rule, but most could not keep pace. Led by Jacob Leisler, the disgruntled leaders took advantage of the fall of James II to strike out at the new order.

The Glorious Revolution in New York sparked not the final drive for power by an aspiring element of the elite, but rather a futile last grasp by a declining one. And of greater importance, the clash within New York's elite was merely the complement to deep-seated antagonisms within the population. When news of the Glorious Revolution reached New York, the opposition leaders there, like their counterparts elsewhere in the colonies, stirred up the inhabitants with the bugaboo of papism, but even when the immediate crisis passed the people of the city remained involved and divided.

This division, based on ethnic diversity, underlay New York's peculiarly modern politics. The schism between the Dutch and the English, supported by their Huguenot allies, allowed voters to respond, on grounds which seemed to be reasonable, to the divisions within the elite. Common Dutch citizens were able to appreciate the enmity of Leisler and his successors against the English and French who were taking control of the community. In contrast, English residents were most likely to oppose a movement born of hostility to them and led by persons who could barely speak their language. The Huguenots, the most recent arrivals in the province, could find little relevant to them in the grievances of the Dutch and naturally aligned themselves with their English associates and benefactors.

In an age when most men could possess the franchise and

politicians did not present programs to win their allegiance, the electorate usually became apathetic. But in a situation where divisions among the leaders could be understood in terms of antagonisms within the heterogeneous population, voters and politicians were united in a novel way. This rapport between leaders and followers joined the possibility of easy identification of friends and adversaries to create rudimentary parties which could translate individually-felt frustrations into a political movement. Aroused and enfranchised, the citizenry of New York City became an important force in politics, and voting became an expression of choice rather than a ratification of authority.

New York's experience in the latter part of the seventeenth century has important implications for the study of democratically-oriented politics in the eighteenth century as well. Historians have not satisfactorily explained the basis of the electorate's response to the factions which played so prominent a role in the years preceding the Revolution. In instances of sectional issues, the presumption of a sectional response is reasonable, but in cases of local divisions, the identification of one contending group as the "popular" party and the other as the "court" party seems inadequate. Popular leaders, after winning election, quickly found virtues in the prerogative power, and former court politicians easily resorted to popular appeals. In any case, voters may not have been affected by such maneuvers. The occurrence of hotly contested elections suggests that even the court party was able to draw considerable popular support.[13]

The existence of party-oriented politics in the eighteenth century may well be explained by divisions within the population

[13] See Alison Gilbert Olson, *Anglo-American Politics, 1660–1775: The Relationship between Parties in England and Colonial America* (New York, 1973); Patricia U. Bonomi, *A Factious People: Politics and Society in Colonial New York* (New York, 1971), p. 122.

similar to those that occurred in the seventeenth. In New York, eighteenth century observers noted that English-Dutch tensions became a serious problem at Albany as the effects of the conquest of 1664 finally reached there. The English, who stereotyped the Dutch as parsimonious and hostile to superior authority, complained that "foreigners . . . who know as yet so little of the English Constitution" could have no love of their country or her liberties. In the 1750s participants in the Livingston-De Lancey dispute in New York City played upon the hostility between Presbyterians and Anglicans. Likewise, in Pennsylvania the struggle of Quaker assembly spokesmen and Anglican supporters of the proprietor may well have fed upon corresponding splits within the population, and both sides vied for the assistance of the bloc votes of German and Scotch-Irish immigrants.[14]

Recognition of the important political role of such cultural factors as ethnicity and religion underscores the significance of the middle colonies in the study of American history. Communities like New York City and Philadelphia, where men of different backgrounds learned to practice the arts of conflict and accommodation, were the locales where deferential politics began to evolve into popular democracy. Conceivably, the lessons which they drew from the process were fundamental to the development of the ideals of pluralism and democracy which the American nation eventually espoused. The possibilities, at least, are worthy of further examination.

[14] Bonomi, *Factious People,* pp. 27, 53. Bonomi attributes the quotation to Adam, Lord Gordon; Milton Klein, ed., *The Independent Reflector* (Cambridge, Mass., 1963); Gary B. Nash, "The Transformation of Urban Politics, 1700–1765," *Journal of American History,* LX (Dec. 1973), 605–32.

❧ *Essay on Sources and Methods*

The most important primary sources for this work were the two tax lists which identify the population of New York City in 1677 and 1703. They made possible the comparison on which this study is based. The published minutes of the Common Council for July 24, 1677 note the assessments of approximately two hundred ninety heads of families. Tax rolls for July, September, and December 1703, and February 1703/4 estimate the value of the houses and estates, or simply the estates of slightly more than a thousand heads of families. All levels of government worked vigorously to make taxation inescapable, so the assessment sheets provide a rather complete tally of the island's residents. The Assembly declared "all and every Inhabitants freeholders and Sojourners . . ." to be subject to levies, and the city's Common Council, angered that some people were reaping benefits without bearing burdens, ordered even "strangers" to pay taxes after one month's residence.[1]

The small size of New York's population in 1677, and the existence of some secondary studies concerning the city at the time of the conquest, made possible the identification of virtually all the persons on the tax rolls for that year. *New Amster-*

[1] *Min. Com. Coun.*, July 24, 1677; Aug. 15, 1684, I, 50–63, 154; Klapper Library, Queens College, City University of New York; "An Act to Enable the City of New York to Relieve the Poor and Defray Their Necessary and Public Charge," July 3, 1695, *Col. Laws*, p. 350.

dam and Its People by J. H. Innes and the *History of New York City* by David T. Valentine were especially helpful.[2] Establishing a base population from the 1703 rolls was more difficult.

The 1703 tax rolls include the names of residents of the Out Ward, which I immediately omitted. This ward comprised the Bowery and Harlem; the latter district was incorporated into the city in 1674, but enjoyed a quasi-independent status and a separate history.[3] The Out Ward, moreover, was a rural area, and treating it in a primarily urban study would have complicated the investigation and might have distorted the results.

Problems in identifying the residents of the city's five central wards forced additional deletions from the 1703 lists. Some entries were illegible, and persons who appeared on only one of the four assessment rolls were considered transient. The final roster contained 876 names. Despite the necessary omissions, this included almost all of the white heads of families and free single adults who left any trace of their existence.

After establishing the population roster for 1703, the next requirement was to gather substantial amounts of information about each person.[4] A census of Manhattan taken in 1703 provided a starting point. Containing many fewer names than the tax list, and available only through an imperfect copy, the census was not suitable as the base list of the study. But it did supply important information for most households, including the name of the master or mistress of the family, and the numbers of "Males from 16 to 60, females, Male Children, female Chil-

[2] New York, 1902; New York, 1853.

[3] James Riker, *Revised History of Harlem* (New York, 1904), is the standard history of the district.

[4] The population roster for 1703, with the available information about each person, forms "Appendix B" of my dissertation, "The Age of Leisler: New York City, 1689–1710: A Social and Demographic Interpretation," Columbia University, 1971.

dren, Male Negros, female Negros, Male Negro Children, female Negro Children, [and] all [persons] above 60.'' Presumably some of the individuals noted as family members were indentured servants, but the lack of available data about this group made further study of them impossible.[5]

The books by Innes and Valentine again proved useful, but genealogies constituted the most important secondary source. Genealogy is a valid tool for the historian, but its bibliography varies greatly in quality. Hagiographers who trace their forebearers back to Adam in a direct line through Jesus Christ and Moses at least entertain us, though at the price of lost research time. More dangerous are amateurs equipped only with enthusiasm and filiopietism; their studies flourished at the beginning of the twentieth century and had strong Social Darwinist overtones. In general, the researcher should limit himself or herself to modern studies by competent professionals. The articles in the New York Genealogical and Biographical Society's *Record* are especially valuable.

Once the 1677 and 1703 population rosters were established, it was possible to delineate the patterns of wealth distribution on Manhattan. The assessors apparently had estimated the value of each resident's property and personal estate at only part of its actual value, so their figures cannot serve as absolute measurements of financial well-being. Yet their evaluations do represent the judgments of informed observers on the relative economic standing of every family within the city.

In order to simplify the use of this data and to emphasize its

[5] ''Census of the City of New York [About the Year 1703],'' *DHNY,* I, 611–24. Dr. O'Callaghan apparently had difficulty deciphering the handwriting of the census takers; for example, the surnames of Francis Goederis, Elias Neau, and Robert Sinclair became Coderos, Now, and Sinkeler, respectively. The original census was destroyed by the 1911 fire at the State Capitol in Albany. O'Callaghan listed 766 names in the East, West, North, South, and Dock Wards.

nature as an estimate of relative rather than of real wealth, the rosters for 1677 and 1703 were translated into scales of economic standing. The basic procedure was the same for both lists and is described in the text.

Assessments on the 1677 list converged in a way that suggested the use of a rough four-section scale for that roster. The much larger population compiled from the 1703 rolls and the more even distribution of the valuations made it possible to create a larger number of intervals for the 1703 roster. The clustering of approximately 20 percent of the population at the low assessment of £5 pointed to the use of a five-interval scale for many computations. In situations where the behavior of persons of middle or upper stations was of special interest, a ten-interval scale was more appropriate.[6]

Use of four intervals for 1677 and five or ten intervals for 1703 impeded comparison of the scales, but this shortcoming was not critical. Indeed, because of the differences in population size and the somewhat impressionistic quality of the data, attempts at direct comparison might have been imprudent. In any case, internal examinations of the scales fully revealed how great a social and economic change occurred in New York City in the latter part of the seventeenth century.

Church records were the best means of identifying the national backgrounds of the people on the lists. The baptismal records of the Dutch Reformed Church were valuable, but the marriage records, which often indicate the birthplaces of the brides and grooms, were especially useful. The register of

[6] The following shows the relationship between an individual's tax for 1677 or amount of evaluation for 1703 and the interval that person would rank in on the scales of wealth. 1677: up to £0.5.6 = 1, up to £0.6 = 2, up to £0.8 = 3, more than £0.8 = 4; 1703: up to £5 = 2, up to £10 = 3, up to £15 = 4, up to £20 = 5, up to £30 = 6, up to £45 = 7, up to £70 = 8, up to £110 = 9, more than £110 = 10.

births, marriages and deaths which the Eglise du Saint-Esprit maintained assisted in the identification of Huguenots. Unfortunately, similar documents for the English are not extant, but the Minutes of the Vestry of Trinity Church served as a partial substitute, and other sources supplemented the data obtained from church records.[7]

Various documents revealed the occupations of persons mentioned on the lists. The freemanship lists, which often noted the specific employment which the enrollee obtained authorization to pursue, were the most obvious source. But virtually every public record in the period, including wills and inventories of estates, court minutes, and deeds, noted the employments or social stations of the persons mentioned.[8]

Of all the occupational groups, merchants were of greatest interest in this study, and customhouse records provided the basic source of information about their activities. According to "An Act for Granting unto His Majesty Several Duties for the Defraying the Publick Charge of the Government . . . ," the mate, master, or purser of "all Ships and Vessels whatsoever,

---

[7] *Coll. NYGBS,* Vols. II and IX; *Coll. HSA;* Min. Ves.; Secretary of State, New York State, *Names of Persons for Whom Marriage Licenses Were Issued by the Secretary of the Province of New York Previous to 1784* (Albany, 1860).

[8] *The Burghers of New Amsterdam and the Freemen of New York 1675–1866,* in the *Coll. NYHS,* Vol. XVIII (1885); *Abstracts of Wills,* in the *Coll. NYHS,* Vols. XXV–XLI (1892–1908). The Klapper Library houses most of the original New York City will libers and the extant inventories of estates. The New-York Historical Society houses additional inventories. The Surrogate's Court in Manhattan maintains copies of the original wills, including those testaments which Klapper Library does not have. The Minutes of the Mayor's Court may be found at the Hall of Records. The Special Collections division at Butler Library, Columbia University, has in its Benjamin Salzer Collection approximately two thousand of the original Mayor's Court pleadings; Klapper Library holds additional ones. The Minutes of the Court of Quarter Sessions of the City of New York are maintained at the library of the Criminal Court.

that shall come to any Port, Creek or Harbour within this Province" had to report "all such parcel or parcels of Merchantize, or other things" on board and swear that the bulk was intact.[9] Julius M. Bloch *et al.* have published in *An Account of Her Majesty's Revenue in the Province of New York, 1701–1709: The Customs Records of Early Colonial New York* the extant portions of these records, including full data on the years 1701 and 1702 which coincided with the later focus of this study.[10]

The customs records yield incomplete data but do provide a good impression of the important patterns of commerce through the port. Statistics on importation are excellent in regard to England, the West Indies, and the Atlantic Islands, less strong for the mainland colonies, and weak in relation to intraprovincial business. Data are also available for the transatlantic fur trade.

Importers paid £2 on each £100 worth of general merchandise, and an additional duty of £5 per £100 worth of Indian goods, including "Duffils, red, blew, and black, Strounds, Blankets, Plains, half thicks, Wollen Stockins, White Ozenbrugs, Mellish Kettles, Hatchets, Hoes, Red Lead, Vermillion, Cotton, Red Kersies, Knives, [and] Indian Habbardasherry." Merchants who dealt with the West Indies and the Atlantic Islands had to pay 4 pence per gallon of "Rum, Brandy, and Distilled beverages" and £2 for "every pipe of Madera, Malmey, Fyall, St. George, Passedo, Canary Mallego, Sherry" and other sweet wines.[11]

---

[9] "An Act for Granting unto His Majesty Several Duties for the Defraying the Publick Charge of the Government after the Time Limitted in an Act Entled, An Act Confirming and Continuing unto Their Majesties the Revenue Established by an Act of the General Assembly for Defraying the Publick and Necessary Charge of the Government, Is Expired," May 15, 1699, *Col. Laws,* p. 422.

[10] Ridgewood, N.J., 1966. The compilers found the data for 1701 and 1702 in Con. Lib., Vol. XXX.

[11] "An Act for Granting Several Duties," *Col. Laws,* p. 420.

Persons who engaged in commerce with other mainland provinces or who operated within the boundaries of New York Colony escaped some of the revenue measures. The legislators evidently hoped to encourage the citizenry to carry their colony's trade, and sought to guarantee its inhabitants every possible access to necessities. Many goods imported from or through nearby settlements were liable to duties, but grains and "any other thing of the Growth and Production of our Neighbouring Collonies," including in part, salt, bricks, fish, sugar, tobacco, cotton, wool, flax, soap, candles, beef, timber, deerskins, bullion, plate, apples and pears, were not taxable. Trade up and down the Hudson River was also free, except for traffic in weapons, lead, and gunpowder.[12]

Export fees were levied on the lucrative transatlantic fur trade. The legislation passed in 1699 did not mention any tax on commerce going from New York to the other mainland colonies, South America, the West Indies, or the Atlantic Islands but did assign duties on the valuable pelts which went primarily to the London market. The rates varied from 9 pence for one whole beaver to 9 pence for twenty-four "Musk Rats." [13]

Customhouse materials contain information on only the imports and exports which passed through the port of New York and do not indicate the total amount of commerce conducted in the city. Few letter books, account ledgers, or other critical documents belonging to early New York merchants are available, so despite their shortcomings the customhouse statistics are the best source of information about the city's merchant class.

The organization of the customs reports, however, makes the task of identifying New York's most important merchants difficult. The records divide commercial activity into four spheres which cannot readily be compared. They note the value of the

[12] *Ibid.*, pp. 420–21.   [13] *Ibid.*, pp. 421–22.

cargo for general merchandise, but only the number of gallons, pipes, and skins for rum, wine, and furs respectively. And although the records reveal the amount of duties paid for all shipments, merchants paid for taxable merchandise according to its value and for rum, wine, and furs according to the number of gallons, pipes, and skins imported or exported. In such a situation any approach employed to rank the merchants in the order of their overall importance encounters risks, but the use of an average score based on their unweighted standings in each of the four major areas seemed least hazardous.

Merchants involved in the importation of general goods, which included a wide range of items from pots and pans to chests with unspecified contents, were ranked according to the total value of the materials which they received during the years 1701 and 1702. Similar procedures, based on the amount of taxes paid by the merchants on rum, wine, and exports during the same period, created rankings for the three remaining areas. Each of the lists was then divided into ten approximately equal parts and the traders on it were assigned a score appropriate to their position in the standings.

Though informative and suggestive, these separate lists of importance were of limited use because they did not indicate the overall importance of each merchant. A fifth, composite scale was more valuable. To create this final standing, individual merchants were ranked according to the combined point totals of the earlier lists. The overall list was then divided into ten approximately equal sections, and each merchant assigned a score, ranging from a low of one to a high of ten, determined by the interval in which he or she fell.[14]

[14] The following shows the relation between total cargo values or duties and the interval of rank in each of the four scales. Goods(Value): Up to £64 = 1, £207 = 2, £417 = 3, £651 = 4, £1119 = 5, £1749 = 6, £2832 = 7, £5793 = 8, £11,573 = 9, £32,711 = 10. Rum(Duty): Up to £7 = 1, £17 = 2,

Use of the unweighted scale may have given inadequate emphasis to the importance of merchants engaged in transatlantic commerce. Trade with England, which required connections and access to large amounts of credit there, was obviously more indicative of a merchant's importance than trade with any other area. The distortion, however, was minimal. Merchants trading with London usually dealt with other ports as well, and their multifaceted activities assured them positions high on the scale of importance. Moreover, the establishment of exportation to England as a category of commerce separate from the importation of goods gave additional recognition to merchants who dealt with that country.

The assessment rolls, used in conjunction with other sources, made it possible to determine the street of residence of most New Yorkers in the 1677 and 1703 populations. The Common Council minutes list the persons mentioned in the 1677 assessment according to street or general area of residence. Valentine's *History* more precisely locates the dwellings of citizens who lived in vaguely defined sections such as the Water Side, which encompassed much of the shoreline surrounding the inhabited districts of the island.

For 1703 the tax rolls are separated into six categories by ward of residence. Detailed comparison of these rolls with New York's land transfer records, which not only note the street location of the property involved, but also identify the owners of adjacent houses and lots, demonstrated that the collectors

---

£23 = 3, £40 = 4, £54 = 5, £68 = 6, £111 = 7, £147 = 8, £319 = 9, £674 = 10. Wine(Duty): Up to £4.7.6 = 2, £16 = 4, £49.6.8 = 6, £180 = 8, £755 = 10. Exports(Duty): Up to £2 = 1, £6 = 2, £11 = 3, £14 = 4, £22 = 5, £33 = 6, £48 = 7, £65 = 8, £91 = 9, £149 = 10. The following shows the relation between total points scored and the interval of rank in the scale. Up to 3 = 2, 6 = 4, 8 = 5, 9 = 6, 12 = 7, 17 = 8, 23 = 9, 40 = 10.

conducted a door-to-door canvass.[15] Accordingly, determining the sites of the residences of most of New York City's 1703 population was relatively easy.

The 1703 assessment rolls also distinguish householders from tenants. A homeowner's residence is described as his or her "house and estate;" a second house is simply called "house." A tenant is noted as having an "estate in" the house of the last mentioned owner. This clear separation made possible a description of the patterns of tenancy at the beginning of the eighteenth century.

Once extracted from the sources, the data from the assessment and land records was combined with the scale of mercantile importance to show the relative importance of Manhattan's streets. Each street was given a score equal to the total of the individual scores of the merchants in residence there. The streets were then ranked.

Publications such as the *Minutes of the Common Council,* the *Journal of the . . . General Assembly,* and the *Journal of the Legislative Council* identify those who held political office.[16] Data drawn from these sources for the years from 1691 to 1710, when the colony and city had continually functioning governmental systems, contributed to the construction of an office-tenure matrix to analyze the concentration of political power in the community. Each major political post was assigned an office-point value reflecting its relative importance; the possible tenure-points varied directly with the lengths of time in office.

---

[15] Con. Lib.; New York City, Water Grants, 1686–1907, Dept. of Real Estate, New York, Liber A.

[16] *Min. Com. Coun.;* New York Colony, *Journal of the Votes and Proceedings of the General Assembly of the Colony of New York, 1691–1765* (New York, 1764–1766); New York Colony, *Journal of the Legislative Council of the Colony of New York, 1691–1775* (Albany, 1861).

Multiplying the office-points for a particular position by the tenure-points of an individual generated the score for each officeholder.[17]

Because construction of a matrix of political influence is inevitably arbitrary, this index has been intentionally designed to err on the side of conservatism. In order to recognize the importance of on-going leadership, it puts a premium on tenure in office. In theory, a person who held a minor post for a prolonged period of time might rank as high as one who briefly enjoyed a major position. But in reality, the lowest-ranking offices had the greatest rates of turnover. That the elite emerged as having held a tremendous proportion of the power in the community despite the bias in the measurement is all the more striking.

Statistics shaped almost every chapter of this study. The text attests to the use of such simple measures as means and medians, but more complex computations were also made. A cross-tabulation program, prepared by the University of California at Los Angeles, was applied to the problems involving the voluminous 1703 data.[18] It helped isolate the social and economic peculiarities of persons who voted, served on juries, held slaves, engaged in commerce, and resided on the particular streets of the city. Analysis of the correlation coefficients, which measure the strength of association between variables, verified the conclusions presented.

A standardized multiple regression program, also prepared by

[17] The office-point relationship was: governor, 10; lieutenant governor, 9; Governor's Council, 8; assembly, 7; judge, 7; mayor, 6; militia colonel, 6; recorder, 6; treasurer, 6; alderman, 5; militia captain, 5; assistant, 4; sheriff, 3; miscellaneous posts, 3; assessor, 2; collector, 1; constable, 1. The tenure-point relationship was: 1–2 years, 1; 3–4 years, 2; etc. As there were only thirteen assemblies held during this period, provincial legislators earned one tenure-point for each assembly in which they sat.

[18] W. J. Dixon, ed., *BMD—Biomedical Computer Programs* (Los Angeles, 1967).

the University of California at Los Angeles, proved to be valuable too, especially in uncovering the ethnic basis of political affiliation.[19] Using dichotomous variables (0,1) made it possible to include categorical as well as continuous variables in the analysis. The test enables the investigator to determine more accurately the most important factor affecting a problem because the partial correlation coefficients generated by the program measure the effect of each variable on the phenomenon only after controlling for the combined effect of the other factors under examination. The program also produces proportions of cumulative variations which show the percentage of the total phenomenon explained by each variable.[20]

Techniques like those used in this study to organize and analyze data can be great assets, but they also have limitations. The regression test employed originated as an aid to biomedical research, but human behavior lacks the constancy and predictability of laboratory materials. Historians, especially those investigating periods where the data is unrefined, cannot expect to explain "statistically" a high percentage of phenomena. Data processing and testing procedures aid historical analysis, but cannot substitute for it. How the historian interprets and makes rational the findings remains a product of his or her intuition, training, and knowledge.

[19] *Ibid.*

[20] The dependent variable Leislerian equaled 0 and Anti-Leislerian equaled 1; ethnic variable Dutch equaled 0 and English/French 1.

# Bibliography

PRIMARY SOURCES

Manuscripts

Personal

Nicholas Bayard Papers, 1698–1710. New-York Historical Society.
William Blathwayt Miscellaneous Papers. New-York Historical Society.
Richard Coote, Earl of Bellomont, Papers. New-York Historical Society.
De Lancey Papers, 1647–1804. New-York Historical Society.
De Peyster Papers, 1677–1878. New-York Historical Society.
Jacobus Van Cortlandt Letter Book, 1698–1700. New-York Historical Society.

Public

London, City of. Account of the Distribution Made to the Poor French Protestant Refugees, of the Money Proceeding Both from the Subscriptions and of the Collection Granted by the King's Most Excellent Majesty, the 31st March 1694. Guidhall Library, London.
New York City. Assessment Rolls, 1703–1704. Microfilm. Klapper Library, Queens College, City University of New York.
——. Conveyance Libers, 1683–1724. Vols. XIII–XXX. Register's Office, Hall of Records, New York.
——. Inventories of Estates. Most of the extant colonial inventories are in Klapper Library, Queens College, City University of New York.
——. Minutes of the Court of Quarter Sessions. Criminal Court Building, New York.
——. Minutes of the Mayor's Court. Hall of Records, New York.
——. Pleas of the Mayor's Court. Special Collections, Butler Library, Columbia University.
——. Water Grants, 1686–1907. 10 libers. Dept. of Real Estate, New York.
——. Wills, 1665–1716. Vol. I–VIII. Most of the originals from the colonial period are in Klapper Library, Queens College, City University of New York. Copies are in the Hall of Records.

New York Colony. Colonial Manuscripts (Miscellaneous). New York State Library, Albany.

New York State. Land Patents, 1680–1751. 6 vols. New York State Library, Albany.

Trinity Church, Corporation of. Minutes of the Vestry. Vol. I (1697–1791). Photocopy. Office of Trinity Church, New York.

Books

Andrews, Charles McLean, ed. *Narratives of the Insurrections, 1675–1690.* New York, 1915.

Bloch, Julius M., Leo Hershkowitz, Kenneth Scott, Constance D. Sherman, eds. *An Account of Her Majesty's Revenue in the Province of New York, 1701–1709: The Customs Records of Early Colonial New York.* Ridgewood, N.J., 1966.

Corwin, Edwin T., and Hugh Hastings, eds. *Ecclesiastical Records of the State of New York.* 8 vols. Albany, 1901.

Dangler, Adolph, ed. *Descriptive Index of the Maps on Record in the Office of the Register of the City and County of New York.* New York, 1875.

Dankers, Jasper, and Peter Sluyter. *Journal of a Voyage to New York and a Tour in Several of the American Colonies in 1679–1680.* Edited by Henry C. Murphy. Brooklyn, N.Y., 1867.

Denton, Daniel. *A Brief Description of New York, Formerly Called New Netherland.* London, 1670. Reprinted Cleveland, 1902.

Donnan, Elizabeth, ed. *Documents Illustrative of the History of the Slave Trade to America.* 3 vols. Washington, D.C., 1932.

Fernow, Berthold. *Calendar of Wills on File and Recorded in the Office of the Secretary of State, 1626–1836.* New York, 1896.

——, ed. *The Records of New Amsterdam from 1653 to 1674.* 7 vols. New York, 1897.

Greene, E. B., and V. D. Harrington, eds. *American Population before the Federal Census of 1790.* New York, 1932.

Hershkowitz, Leo, ed. *Wills of Early New York Jews, 1704–1799.* New York, 1967.

Hinton, R. W. K., ed. *The Port Books of Boston, 1601–1640.* Vol. L of the *Publications of the Lincoln Record Society.* Hereford, Eng., 1956.

Jameson, J. Franklin, ed. *Narratives of New Netherland, 1609–1664.* New York, 1909.

Klein, Milton, ed. *The Independent Reflector.* Cambridge, Mass., 1963.

Lawson, John D., ed. *American State Trials.* Vol. X. St. Louis, 1918.

Miller, John. *Description of the Province and City of New York . . . 1695.* London, 1843.

Miller, Perry, ed. *The American Puritans.* New York, 1956.

Morris, Richard B., ed. *Select Cases of the Mayor's Court of New York City, 1674–1874*. Washington, D.C., 1935.

New York City. *Abstracts of [New York] Wills*. Vols. XXV–XLI of the *New-York Historical Society Collections*. New York, 1892–1908.

——. *Baptisms from 1639 to 1730 in the Dutch Reformed Church: New Amsterdam and New York City*. Vol. II of the *New York Genealogical and Biographical Society Collections*. New York, 1901. Reprinted Upper Saddle River, N.J., 1968.

——. *The Burghers of New Amsterdam and the Freemen of New York, 1675–1866*. Vol. XVIII of the *New-York Historical Society Collections*. New York, 1885.

——. *Court Records, 1680–1682, 1693–1701*. Vol. XLV of the *New-York Historical Society Collections*. New York, 1912.

——. *Indentures of Apprenticeship, February 19, 1694 to January 29, 1707*. Vol. XVIII of the *New-York Historical Society Collections*, pp. 563–622. New York, 1885.

——. *Marriages from 1639 to 1801 in the Reformed Dutch Church: New Amsterdam and New York City*. Vol. IX of the *New York Genealogical and Biographical Society Collections*. New York, 1940.

——. *Minutes of the Common Council of the City of New York, 1675–1776*. 8 vols. Edited by Herbert Levi Osgood. New York, 1905.

——. *Tax Lists of the City of New York, December 1695–July 1699*. Vols. XLIII and XLIV of the *New-York Historical Society Collections*. New York, 1910–1911.

New York Colony. *Calendar of Council Minutes, 1668–1783*. (New York State Library, Bulletin 58). Albany, 1902.

——. *The Colonial Laws of New York, from the Year 1664 to the Revolution*. 5 vols. Albany, 1894.

——. *Documents Relating to the Administration of Leisler*. Vol. I of the *New-York Historical Society Collections*, pp. 237–426. New York, 1868.

——. *Journal of the Legislative Council of the Colony of New York, 1691–1775*. 2 vols. Albany, 1861.

——. *Journal of the Votes and Proceedings of the General Assembly of the Colony of New York, 1691–1765*. 2 vols. New York, 1764–1766.

New York County. *Court of Lieutenancy: Records, 1686–1696*. Vol. XIII of the *New-York Historical Society Collections*. New York, 1880.

New York State. Comptroller. *List of Patents of Lands, etc., to Be Sold in January 1822 for Arrears of Quit Rent*. Albany, 1822.

——. Secretary of State. *Calendar of New York Colonial Manuscripts: Indorsed Land Papers in the Office of the Secretary of State of New York, 1643–1803*. Albany, 1864.

——. ——. *Names of Persons for Whom Marriage Licenses Were Issued by the Secretary of the Province of New York Previous to 1784.* Albany, 1860.

———. ———. *Supplementary List of Marriage Licenses.* Albany, 1898.

O'Callaghan, Edmund B., ed. *Documentary History of the State of New York.* 4 vols. Albany, 1849–1851.

———. *Documents Relative to the Colonial History of the State of New York.* 15 vols. Albany, 1856–1887.

———. *Voyages of the Slavers "St. John" and "Arms of Amsterdam," 1659 and 1663.* Albany, 1867.

Post, J. J., ed. *Abstract of Title of Kip's Bay Farm in the City of New York.* 3 vols. New York, 1894.

———. *Index of Wills Proved in the Supreme Court, Court of Common Pleas, County Court, and Court of Probate, and on File in the Office of the Clerk of the Court of Appeals.* New York, 1899.

Seymann, Jerrold, ed. *Colonial Charters, Patents, and Grants to the Communities Comprising the City of New York.* New York, 1939.

Still, Bayrd, ed. *Mirror for Gotham: New York City as Seen by Contemporaries from Dutch Days to the Present.* New York, 1956.

Stokes, I. N. P., ed. *The Iconography of Manhattan Island, 1498–1909.* 6 vols. New York, 1915–1928.

Tuttle, H. C., ed. *Abstracts of Farm Titles in the City of New York.* 3 vols. New York, 1868.

Winship, George, ed. *The Journal of Madame Knight.* Boston, 1920.

Wittmeyer, [Rev.] Alfred V., ed. *Registers of the Births, Marriages, and Deaths of the "Eglise Françoise à la Nouvelle York," from 1683 to 1804.* Vol. I of the *Collections of the Huguenot Society of America.* New York, 1886.

Articles

Andrews, Wayne, ed. "A Glance at New York in 1697: The Travel Diary of Dr. Benjamin Bullivant," *New-York Historical Society Quarterly,* XL (Jan. 1956), 55–73.

Lodwick, Charles. "New York in 1692," *New-York Historical Society Collections,* 2d ser., II (1849), 241–50.

New-York Historical Society. "Old New York Inventories of Estate," *New-York Historical Society Quarterly Bulletin,* VI (Jan. 1923), 130–37; VIII (July 1924), 43–46.

Scott, Kenneth, ed. "Early New York Inventories of Estates," *National Genealogical Society Quarterly,* LIII (June 1965), 133–43.

———. "New York Inventories, 1666–1775," *National Genealogical Society Quarterly,* LIV (Dec. 1966), 246–59.

———. "New York Marriage Licenses, 1639–1706," *New York Genealogical and Biographical Record,* XCVIII (Jan. 1967), 1–10, (Apr. 1967), 83–91.

Selyns, [Dominie] Henricus. "List of Members of the Dutch Reformed Church in New York in 1686: Arranged According to the Streets of the City," in the *Yearbook of the Holland Society*. New York, 1916, pp. 1–37.

SECONDARY SOURCES

Genealogies

Books

Abbott, John Howard. *The Courtright (Kortright) Family*. New York, 1922.

Atterbury, Mrs. Anson Phelps. *The Bayard Family*. Baltimore, 1928.

Banker, Howard James. *A Partial History and Genealogy of the Bancker or Banker Families of America*. Rutland, Vt., 1909.

Bartow, Evelyn B. *Bartow Genealogy*. Baltimore, 1878.

Belknap, Waldron Phoenix, Jr. *The De Peyster Genealogy*. Boston, 1956.

Benson, Charles B. *Abraham Van Deursen and Many of His Decendants, 1635–1901*. New York, 1901.

Bergen, Teunis G. *The Bergen Family; or, The Descendants of Hans Hansen Bergen, One of the Early Settlers of New York and Brooklyn, Long Island*. New York, 1866.

Blauvelt, Louis L. *The Blauvelt Family Genealogy*. New York, 1957.

Bookstäver, J. E. *The Willet Genealogy*. Binghamton, N.Y.,1906.

Briggs, Samuel. *The Book of the Varian Family*. Cleveland, 1881.

Čapek, Thomas. *Augustine Herrman of Bohemia Manor*. Prague, Czechoslovakia, 1930.

Carpenter, Daniel Hooghland. *History and Genealogy of the Hoagland Family in America, 1636–1891*. New York, 1891.

Champine, Emojene Demarest. *Jacques Le Roux, the French Huguenot*. Minneapolis, 1939.

Clarkson, William. The Clarksons of New York. 2 vols. New York, 1875.

Cole, David. *Isaac Kool (Cool or Cole) and Catherine Serven: Their Descendants Complete to May 1, 1876; Also Their American Ancestors from the Settlement of New York City*. New York, 1876.

Corson, Orville. *Three Hundred Years with the Corson Family in America*. 2 vols. Middletown, Ohio, 1939.

Crosby, Ernest H. *The Rutgers Family of New York*. New York, 1886.

Davenport, Marion Gertrude. *A Colonial History and Genealogy of the Bickleys, Gardners, Polegreens, Millers, Dottins, Husbands*. Rochester, N.Y., 1942.

De Forest, J. W. *The De Forests of Avesnes (and of New Netherland)*. New Haven, Conn., 1900.

De Forest, L. Effingham. *The Van Cortlandt Family*. New York, 1930.

De Forest, Mrs. Robert W. *A Walloon Family in America.* 2 vols. New York, 1914.

De La Mater, La Fayette. *Genealogy of the Descendants of Claude Le Maitre (Delamater).* Albany, 1882.

Demarest Family Association (Voorhis D. Demarest, Pres.). *The Demarest Family.* 2 vols. New York, 1964.

De Riemer, W. E. *The De Riemer Family.* New York, 1905.

De Voe, Thomas F. *Genealogy of the De Veaux Family.* New York, 1885.

Donaldson, Frances Flaacke. *The Lockman and Flaacke Families of Early New York.* Washington, D.C., 1965.

Duyckinck, Whitehead Cornell, and John Cornell. *The Duyckinck and Allied Families.* New York, 1908.

Fish, Stuyvesant. *Anthon Genealogy.* New York, 1930.

Flint, Martha Bockée. *The Bockée Family, 1641–1896.* Poughkeepsie, N.Y., 1897.

Fox, Dixon Ryan. *Caleb Heathcote.* New York, 1926.

Frost, Josephine C. *Ancestors of Henry Rogers Winthrop and His Wife Alice Woodward Babock.* New York, 1927.

——. *The Strang Genealogy.* Brooklyn, N.Y., 1915.

Gordon, William Seton. *Gabriel Ludlow and His Descendants.* [New York, 1919].

Gray, Maria Sabina (Bogardus). *A Genealogical History of the Ancestors and Descendants of General Robert Bogardus.* Boston, 1927.

Hamm, Margherita A. *Famous Families of New York.* 2 vols. New York, 1902.

Heck, Earl L. W. *Augustine Herrman.* Richmond, Va., 1941.

Honeyman, A. Van Doren. *Joannes Nevius and His Descendants, A.D. 1627–1900.* Plainfield, N.J., 1900.

Johnson, R. Winder. *Winders of America.* Philadelphia, 1902.

Jones, Charles Henry. *Genealogy of the Rodman Family, 1620 to 1886.* Philadelphia, 1886.

Kip, Frederick Ellsworth. *History of the Kip Family in America.* Morristown, N.J., 1928.

Latourette, Lyman E. *La Tourette Annals in America.* Portland, Oregon, 1954.

Lawrence, Thomas. *Historical Genealogy of the Lawrence Family.* New York, 1858.

Many, Dorothy Jones. *41 First Cousins: A History of Some Descendants of Jean Many, French Huguenot.* West Hartford, Conn., 1961.

Marston, Nathan Washington. *The Marston Genealogy.* South Lubec, Maine, 1888.

Miller, Myrtle Hardenbergh. *The Hardenbergh Family*. New York, 1958.

Moffat, R. Burnham. *The Barclays of New York, 1904*.

Morris, John E. *The Bontecou Genealogy*. Hartford, Conn., 1885.

Munsell, Claude G. *The Lansing Family*. [New York], 1916.

Nelson, William. *Edward Antill, A New York Merchant of the Seventeenth Century and His Descendants*. Paterson, N.J., 1899.

Nicoll, Maud Churchill. *The Earliest Cuylers in Holland and America*. New York, 1912.

Opdyke, Charles Wilson. *The Op Dyck Genealogy*. Albany, 1884.

Park, N. Grier, comp., and Donald Lines Jacobus, ed. *The Ancestry of Lorenzo Ackley and His Wife Emma Arabella Bosworth*. Woodstock, Vt., 1960.

Pelletreau, William S. *Record of the Pelletreau Family*. n.p., 1913.

Perrin, Anna Falconer, and Mary Falconer Perrin Meeker. *The Allied Families of Purdy, Fauconnier, Archer, Perrin*. New York, 1911.

Pool, David de Sola. *Portraits Etched in Stone: Early Jewish Settlers, 1682–1831*. New York, 1952.

Provost, Andrew J. *Biographical and Genealogical Notes of the Provost Family from 1545 to 1895*. New York, 1895.

Purple, Edwin Ruthven. *Contribution to the History of Ancient Families of New Amsterdam and New York*. New York, 1881.

———. *Genealogical Notes Relating to Lieut.-Gov. Jacob Leisler and His Family Connections in New York*. New York, 1877.

Purple, Samuel S. *Bradford Family: Genealogical Memorials of William Bradford, the Printer*. New York, 1873.

Quackenbush, Adriana Suydam. *The Quackenbush Family in Holland and America*. Paterson, N.J., 1909.

Runk, Emma Ten Broeck. *The Ten Broeck Genealogy*. New York, 1897.

Ryerson, Albert Winslow. *The Ryerson Genealogy*. Chicago, 1916.

Schermerhorn, Richard, Jr. *Schermerhorn Genealogy and Family Chronicle*. New York, 1914.

Schuyler, G. W. *Colonial New York: Philip Schuyler and His Family*. 2 vols. New York, 1885.

Spooner, Walter W., ed. *Historic Families of America*. New York, 1907.

Stanwood, James Rindge. *The Direct Ancestry of the Late Jacob Wendell*. Boston, 1882.

Talcott, S. V., comp. *Genealogical Notes of New York and New England Families*. Albany, 1883.

Ten Eyck, Albert. *Ten Eyck Family Record*. N.p., n.d.

Townsend, Annette. *The Walton Family of New York, 1630–1940*. Philadelphia, 1945.

Van Deusen, Albert Harrison. *The Van Deursen Family*. 2 vols. New York, 1912.

Van Gelder, Arthur P. *Early Van Gelder Families in the United States of America*. Wilmington, Del., 1945.

Van Rensselaer, Mrs. Sarah Rogers. *Ancestral Sketches and Records of Olden Times*. New York, 1882.

Van Winkle, Daniel. *A Genealogy of the Van Winkle Family*. Jersey City, N.J., 1913.

Ver Planck, William Edward. *The History of Abraham Isaacse Ver Planck, and His Male Descendants in America*. Fishkill Landing, N.Y., 1892.

Ver Planck, William Gordon. *The First Church Marriage in the Colony of New York: Van Borsum–Hendricks*. New York, 1896.

Viele, Kathlyne Knickerbocker. *Viele Records, 1613–1913*. New York, 1913.

Vincent, Anna M. *The Vincent Family: Descendants of Adrian Vincent*. Millbrook, N.Y., 1959.

Warner, Peter Roome. *Descendants of Peter Willemse Roome*. New York, 1883.

Weisse, Mrs. John A. *A History of the Bethune Family Together with a Sketch of the Faneuil Family*. New York, 1884.

Westervelt, Walter T. *Genealogy of the Westervelt Family*. New York, 1905.

Whittelsey, Charles Barney. *The Roosevelt Genealogy, 1649–1902*. Hartford, Conn., 1902.

Whittemore, Henry. *The Abeel and Allied Families*. New York, 1899.

Wynkoop, Richard. *Wynkoop Genealogy in the United States of America*. New York, 1904.

Articles

The following have appeared in the *New York Genealogical and Biographical Record:*

Bulloch, J. G. B., and Arthur Adams. "Genealogical Notes Relating to Warnaer Wessels and His Descendants," XLIV (Oct. 1913), 322–34.

Carpenter, Daniel H. "New York's First Mayor," XXVIII (Oct. 1897), 190–96.

Comstock, Samuel Willett. "The Van Ranst Family of New York," LVIII (Oct. 1927), 302–18.

Delafield, John Ross. "Walter Thong of New York and His Forefathers," LXXXIII (Oct. 1952), 196–204.

George, Henry Waterman. "The Ten Eyck Family in New York," LXIII (Apr. 1932), 152–62 (July 1932), 269–85, (Oct. 1932), 321–34.

[Greene, Richard H.]. "Genealogy of the Family Named Brasier, Brasher, Breser, Bresart, Bradejor," XXVII (Jan. 1896), 37–42.

Mesereau, Henry Lawrence. "Mesereau Family Genealogy," XXVII (Oct. 1896), 195–97.

Moore, C. B. "English and Dutch Intermarriages," IV (Jan. 1873), 13–20, (July 1873), 127–39.

O'Callaghan, Edmund B. "John Chambers; One of the Justices of the Supreme Court of the Province of New York," III (Apr. 1872), 57–62.

———. "Lancaster Symes," V (Jan. 1874), 1–3.

Pearson, Jonathan. "Contributions to the Ancient Dutch Families of New York," II (Jan. 1871), 22–24 (Apr. 1871), 68–70 (July 1871), 139–41, (Oct. 1871), 190–92.

Randolph, Howard S. F. "The Elsworth Family of New York, with the Related Families of Rommen–Romme–Van Langstraat and Roome," LXIV (Apr. 1933), 154–66, (July 1933), 255–67.

———. "The Hardenbrook Family," LXX (Apr. 1939), 128–33 (Oct. 1939), 373–78.

———. "Jacob Boelen, Goldsmith, of New York and His Family Circle," LXXII (Oct. 1941), 265–94.

———. "The Kiersteade Family," LXV (July 1934), 224–33 (Oct. 1934), 329–38.

———. "The Lewis Family of New York and Poughkeepsie," LX (Apr. 1929), 131–42 (July 1929), 245–54.

———. "The Rommen–Romme–Van Langstraat Family and the Roome Family: Showing Connections between These Two Families and the Elsworth Family of New York City," LXIV (Oct. 1933), 330–41.

———. "The Van Zandt Family of New York City," LXI (Oct. 1930), 317–46; LXII (Apr. 1931), 160–73.

Scott, Kenneth. "The French Refugee Pierre Le Grand of New York City," XCI (Jan. 1960), 1–4.

Spell, Mrs. John M. "The Van Barkelo Family in America," LXXXIV (Apr. 1953), 70–81, (Oct. 1953), 196–207.

Spenser-Mounsey, Creighton. "The Carmer Family of New York: Abraham Kermer and Some of His Descendants," LXI (Oct. 1930), 356–73.

———. "The Mesier Family of New Amsterdam and Wappingers Falls, New York," LVIII (Apr. 1927), 172–80.

Totten, John Reynolds. "Marston Notes," LX (July 1929), 274–78.

———. "Van Beeck Family Notes," LXIV (July 1933), 229–43, (Oct. 1933), 367–87.

Van Deusen, Robert Thompson. "Wendover Family," XXVI (Oct. 1895), 178–85.

Van Sahler, Louis Hasbrouck. "The Early Generations of the Van Deusen Family in America," XXX (Jan. 1899), 46–49, (Apr. 1899), 101–5, (July 1899), 152–58, (Oct. 1899), 205–8; XXXI (Jan. 1900), 55–56.

Van Wagenen, Gerrit. "Early Settlers of Ulster County, New York: The Marsten Family," XX (Oct. 1889), 171–74.

Articles in other magazines include:

Baird, Charles W. "The Birthplace and Parentage of Jacob Leisler," *Magazine of American History,* II (Aug. 1878), 93–95.

——. "Pierre Daillé, the First Huguenot Pastor of New York," *Magazine of American History,* I (Feb. 1877), 91–97.

Lamb, Mrs. Martha J. "The Career and Times of Nicholas Bayard," *Proceedings of the Huguenot Society of America,* II (Apr. 1888–Apr. 1891), 22–57.

Lamoureux, A. J. "André Lamoureux: The Huguenot Emigrant and Family," *The Lamoureux Record,* no. 1 (Oct. 1919).

O'Callaghan, Edmund B. "David Jamison, Attorney-General of the Province of New York, 1710," *Magazine of American History,* I (Jan. 1877), 21–24.

Pargellis, Stanley M. "Jacob Leisler," in the *Dictionary of American Biography.* New York, 1933, VI, 156–57.

Manuscripts

All these manuscripts are available at the New York Genealogical and Biographical Society:

Ackerman, Herbert S. "The Descendants of Jan Pieter Haring." Ridgewood, N.J., 1952. Mimeographed.

Smith, Mary Hart. "The Sloat Family of New Amsterdam." Ontario, Calif., 1941. Typewritten.

Thomas, Howard A. "Noxon Family: Early Generations in New Amsterdam and Dutchess County, New York." 1951. Typewritten.

Viele, Kathlyne Knickerbocker. "Genealogy of the Ackerman Family." Revised and typed by Ellen H. Smith. 1922.

Vredenburgh, William R. "Genealogy of the Vredenburgh Family in North America." Springfield, Ill., 1956. Lithoprint with typewritten editions.

Williams, C. S. "Christian Barentsen Van Horne and His Descendants." New York, 1911. Written from typed copy.

——. "Jan Cornelis Van Horne and His Descendants." New York, 1912. Written from typed copy.

——. "Joris Janzen Van Horne and His Descendants." New York, 1911. Written from typed copy.

General Histories

Books

Adams, Charles McLean. *The Colonial Period of American History.* 4 vols. New Haven, 1937.

Bailyn, Bernard. *The Ideological Origins of the American Revolution.* Cambridge, Mass., 1965.

——. *The New England Merchants in the Seventeenth Century.* Cambridge, Mass., 1955.

——, and Lotte Bailyn. *Massachusetts Shipping, 1697–1714: A Statistical Study.* Cambridge, Mass., 1959.

Baird, Charles W. *History of the Huguenot Emigration to America.* 2 vols. New York, 1885. Reprinted Baltimore, 1966.

Banner, James M., Jr. *To the Hartford Convention: The Federalists and the Origins of Party Politics in Massachusetts, 1789–1815.* New York, 1969.

Barber, Bernard. *Social Stratification.* New York, 1957.

Barnes, Viola F. *The Dominion of New England.* New Haven, 1923. Reprinted New York, 1960.

Bayer, Henry G. *The Belgians: The First Settlers in New York and in the Middle States.* New York, 1925.

Bell, H. E., and R. L. Ollard, eds. *Historical Essays, 1600–1750: Presented to David Ogg.* London, 1963.

Benson, Lee. *The Concept of Jacksonian Democracy: New York as a Test Case.* Princeton, N.J., 1961.

Berrian, William. *An Historical Sketch of Trinity Church, New York.* New York, 1847.

Blalock, Hubert M., Jr. *Social Statistics.* New York, 1960.

Bloom, Herbert I. *The Economic Activities of the Jews of Amsterdam in the Seventeenth and Eighteenth Centuries.* Williamsport, Pa., 1937.

Bonomi, Patricia U. *A Factious People: Politics and Society in Colonial New York.* New York, 1971.

Booth, Mary Louise. *History of the City of New York.* New York, 1859.

Brodhead, John Romeyn. *History of the State of New York.* New York, 1853.

Bushman, Richard L. *From Puritan to Yankee: Character and the Social Order in Connecticut, 1690–1775.* Cambridge, Mass., 1967.

Carr, Lois Green, and David William Jordan. *Maryland's Revolution of Government, 1689–1692.* Ithaca, N.Y., 1974.

Chapelle, Howard I. *The History of American Sailing Ships.* New York, 1935.

Chevalier, Louis. *Classes laborieuses et classes dangereuses à Paris pendant la première moitié du xixᵉ siècle.* Paris, 1958.

Corwin, Edward T. *A History of the Reformed Church, Dutch, the Reformed Church, German, and the Moravian Church in the United States.* New York, 1895.

Cunningham, Noble. *The Jeffersonian Republicans.* 2 vols. Chapel Hill, N.C., 1957–1963.

Daly, Charles Patrick. *History of the Court of Common Pleas for the City and County of New York*. New York, 1855.

———. *The Nature, Extent and History of the Jurisdiction of the Surrogate's Court of the State of New York*. New York, 1863.

———. *The Settlement of the Jews in North America*. New York, 1893.

Demos, John. *A Little Commonwealth: Family Life in Plymouth Colony*. New York, 1970.

Dix, Morgan. *History of the Parish of Trinity Church of the City of New York*. 4 vols. New York, 1898–1906.

Dixon, W. J., ed. *BMD—Biomedical Computer Programs*. Los Angeles, 1967.

Dollar, Charles M., and Richard J. Jensen. *Historian's Guide to Statistics*. New York, 1971.

Douglas, Paul H. *American Apprenticeship and Industrial Education*. New York, 1921.

Durand, Edward Dana. *The Finances of New York City*. New York, 1898.

Earle, Alice Morse. *Colonial Days in Old New York*. New York, 1896.

Edwards, George W. *New York as an Eighteenth Century Municipality: 1731 to 1776*. New York, 1917.

Ellis, Edward Robb. *The Epic of New York City*. New York, 1966.

Ensko, Stephen G. C. *American Silversmiths and Their Mark, 1650–1850*. New York, 1922.

Evjen, John O. *Scandinavian Immigrants in New York, 1630–1674*. Minneapolis, 1916.

Fischer, David H. *The Revolution of American Conservatism: The Federalist Party in the Era of Jeffersonian Democracy*. New York, 1965.

Fiske, John. *The Dutch and Quaker Colonies in America*. 2 vols. Boston, 1899.

Flick, Alexander C., ed. *History of the State of New York*. 10 vols. New York, 1933–1937. Reprinted Port Washington, N.Y., 1962.

Fontaine, Paul R. *Les Établissements maritime rochelais: passé, présent, avenir*. La Rochelle, Fr., 1929.

Fowler, Robert Ludlow. *History of the Law of Real Property in New York: An Essay Introductory to the Study of the New York Revised Statutes*. New York, 1895.

Freund, Miriam K. *Jewish Merchants in Colonial America*. New York, 1939.

George, M. Dorothy. *London Life in the Eighteenth Century*. New York, 1925. Reprinted New York, 1965.

Glass, D. V. *London Inhabitants within the Walls, 1695*. London, 1966.

———, and D. E. C. Eversley, eds. *Population in History: Essays in Historical Demography*. Chicago, 1965.

Goebel, Julius, and T. Raymond Naughton. *Law Enforcement in Colonial New York: A Study in Criminal Procedure.* New York, 1944.

Gordon, Milton M. *Social Class in American Sociology.* Durham, N.C., 1958.

Greven, Philip J., Jr. *Four Generations: Population, Land, and Family in Colonial Andover, Massachusetts.* Ithaca, N.Y., 1970.

Hall, Michael G. *Edward Randolph and the American Colonies.* Chapel Hill, N.C., 1960.

Hamlin, Paul M. *Legal Education in Colonial New York.* New York, 1939.

Hamlin, Paul M., and Charles E. Baker. *Supreme Court of Judicature of the Province of New York, 1691–1704.* Vol. I: *Introduction.* Vol. II: *The Minutes, Annotated.* Vol. III: *Biographical Dictionary.* New York, 1959.

Hansen, Chadwick. *Witchcraft at Salem.* New York, 1969.

Harris, Marshall. *Origin of the Land Tenure System in the United States.* Ames, Iowa, 1953.

Headley, J. T. *The Great Riots of New York, 1712 to 1873.* New York, 1873.

Hecht, J. Jean. *The Domestic Servant Class in Eighteenth Century England.* London, 1956.

Hobsbawm, E. J. *Primitive Rebels: Studies in Archaic Forms of Social Movement in the Nineteenth and Twentieth Centuries.* New York, 1959.

Hoffman, Murray. *Treatise on the Estate and Rights of the Corporation of the City of New York.* 2 vols. New York, 1862.

Innes, J. H. *New Amsterdam and Its People.* New York, 1902.

Johnson, Herbert A. *The Law Merchant and Negotiable Instruments in Colonial New York, 1664–1730.* Chicago, 1963.

Judd, Jacob, and Irwin Polishook, eds. *Aspects of Early New York Society and Politics.* Tarrytown, N.Y., 1973.

Kemp, W. W. *The Support of Schools in Colonial New York by the Society for the Propagation of the Gospel* (Teachers College Contributions to History, no. 56). New York, 1913.

Kessler, Henry H., and Eugene Rachlis. *Peter Stuyvesant and His New York.* New York, 1959.

Kip, William Ingraham. *The Olden Time in New York.* New York, 1872.

Labaree, Leonard W. *Conservatism in Early American History.* New York, 1948.

———. *Royal Government in America: A Study of the British Colonial System before 1783.* New York, 1930. Reprinted New York, 1964.

Lamb, Martha Joanna, and B. Reade. *History of the City of New York.* 3 vols. New York, 1877–1896.

Laslett, Peter. *The World We Have Lost.* New York, 1965.

Lauber, A. W. *Indian Slavery in Colonial Times.* (Columbia Studies in History, Economy, and Public Law, Vol. LIV, no. 3). New York, 1913.

Leder, Lawrence. *Robert Livingston, 1654–1728, and the Politics of Colonial New York.* Chapel Hill, N.C., 1961.

Ledley, Wilson V. *New Netherland Families.* New York, 1958.

Lilly, Edward P. *The Colonial Agents of New York and New Jersey.* Washington, D.C., 1936.

Lockridge, Kenneth. *A New England Town, The First Hundred Years: Dedham, Massachusetts, 1636–1736.* New York, 1970.

Lossing, Benson J. *History of the City of New York.* New York, 1884.

Lovejoy, David S. *The Glorious Revolution in America, 1660–1692.* New York, 1972.

McKee, Samuel. *Labor in Colonial New York, 1664–1776.* New York, 1935. Reprinted Port Washington, N.Y., 1965.

McManus, Edgar J. *A History of Negro Slavery in New York.* Syracuse, N.Y., 1966.

Main, Jackson T. *Political Parties before the Constitution.* Chapel Hill, N.C., 1973.

Miller, V. Isabelle. *Silver by New York Makers: Late Seventeenth Century to 1900.* New York, 1937.

Morris, Richard B. *Government and Labor in Early America.* New York, 1946. Reprinted New York, 1965.

——. *Studies in the History of American Law: With Special Reference to the Seventeenth and Eighteenth Centuries.* New York, 1930.

Morrison, John H. *History of New York Shipyards.* New York, 1909.

Nash, S. P. *Anneke Jans Bogardus; Her Farm and How It Became the Property of Trinity Church.* New York, 1896.

Nissenson, S. G. *The Patroon's Domain.* New York, 1937.

O'Callaghan, Edmund B. *The History of New Netherland; or, New York under the Dutch.* 2 vols. New York, 1846–1848.

Olson, Alison Gilbert. *Anglo-American Politics, 1660–1775: The Relationship between Parties in England and Colonial America.* New York, 1973.

Osgood, Herbert Levi. *The American Colonies in the Eighteenth Century.* 4 vols. New York, 1924.

——. *The American Colonies in the Seventeenth Century.* 3 vols. New York, 1904. Reprinted Gloucester, Mass., 1957.

Pares, Richard. *Yankees and Creoles: The Trade between North America and the West Indies before the American Revolution.* New York, 1956.

Parkinson, C. Northcote, ed. *The Trade Winds: A Study of British Overseas Trade during the French Wars, 1793–1815.* London, 1948.

Pelletreau, William S. *Early New York Houses with Historical and Genealogical Notes.* New York, 1900.

Peterson, Arthur Everett. *New York as an Eighteenth Century Municipality: Prior to 1731.* New York, 1917.

Porter, Kenneth Wiggins. *The Jacksons and the Lees: Two Generations of Massachusetts Merchants, 1765–1884*. 2 vols. Cambridge, Mass., 1937.

Post, J. J. *Old Streets, Roads, Lanes, Piers, and Wharves of New York, Showing the Former and Present Names*. New York, 1882.

Powell, Sumner C. *Puritan Village: The Formation of a New England Town*. Middletown, Conn., 1963.

[Reformed Protestant Dutch Church]. *Historical Sketch of the Origin and Organization of the Reformed Church in America and of the Collegiate Church of the City of New York*. New York, 1899.

Reich, Jerome R. *Leisler's Rebellion: A Study of Democracy in New York, 1664–1720*. Chicago, 1953.

Riker, James. *Revised History of Harlem*. New York, 1904.

Robinson, John, and George F. Dow. *The Sailing Ships of New England, 1607–1907*. Salem, Mass., 1922. Reprinted Westminster, Md., 1953.

Rudé, George F. *The Crowd in History: A Study of Popular Disturbances in France and England, 1730–1848*. New York, 1964.

Scott, Kenneth, comp. *Gold and Silver in 17th Century New York Inventories*. New York, 1966.

Scoville, J. A. *The Old Merchants of New York City*. 4 vols. New York, 1863–1866.

Seybolt, Robert Francis. *Apprenticeship and Apprenticeship Education in Colonial New England and New York*. New York, 1917.

Smith, William. *History of New York, from the First Discovery to the Year M.DCC. XXXII . . . with a Continuation, from the Year 1732, to the Commencement of the Year 1814*. Albany, 1814.

Spenser, Charles W. *Phases of Royal Government in New York, 1691–1719*. Columbus, Ohio, 1905.

Steele, Ian Kenneth. *The Politics of Colonial Policy: The Board of Trade in Colonial Administration, 1696–1720*. Oxford, Eng., 1968.

Sydnor, Charles S. *American Revolutionaries in the Making*. New York, 1965.

Thernstrom, Stephan. *Poverty and Progress: Social Mobility in a Nineteenth-Century City*. Cambridge, Mass., 1964.

Thrupp, Sylvia. *The Merchant Class of Medieval London, 1300–1500*. Chicago, 1948.

Tolles, Frederick B. *Meeting House and Counting House: The Quaker Merchants of Colonial Philadelphia, 1682–1763*. New York, 1948.

Valentine, David T. *History of the City of New York*. New York, 1853.

Van Rensselaer, Mariana Griswold (Mrs. Schuyler). *History of the City of New York in the Seventeenth Century*. 2 vols. New York, 1909.

Waller, G. M. *Samuel Vetch: Colonial Enterpriser*. Chapel Hill, N.C., 1960.

Bibliography

Washburn, Wilcomb E. *The Governor and the Rebel: A History of Bacon's Rebellion in Virginia*. Chapel Hill, N.C., 1957.

Werner, Edgar A. *Civil List and Constitutional History of the Colony and State of New York*. Albany, 1891.

White, Philip L. *The Beekmans of New York in Politics and Commerce, 1647–1877*. New York, 1956.

Wilson, James Grant. *The Memorial History of the City of New York*. 4 vols. New York, 1893.

Wood, Gordon S. *The Creation of the American Republic, 1776–1787*. Chapel Hill, N.C., 1969.

Wrigley, E. A., ed. *An Introduction to English Historical Demography from the Sixteenth to the Nineteenth Century*. London, 1966.

Young, James S. *The Washington Community, 1800–1828*. New York, 1966.

Zuckerman, Michael. *Peaceable Kingdoms: New England Towns in the Eighteenth Century*. New York, 1970.

Articles

Andrews, J. H. "Two Problems in the Interpretation of the Port Books," *Economic History Review*, 2d ser., IX (1956), 119–22.

Bailyn, Bernard. "Communications and Trade: The Atlantic in the Seventeenth Century," *Journal of Economic History*, XIII (Fall 1953), 378–87.

——. "Politics and Social Structure in Virginia," in James M. Smith, ed., *Seventeenth-Century America*. Chapel Hill, N.C., 1959, pp. 90–115.

Barbour, Violet. "Dutch and English Merchant Shipping in the Seventeenth Century," *Economic History Review*, 1st ser., II (Jan. 1930), 261–90.

Baxter, W. T. "Accounting in Colonial America," in A. C. Littleton and B. S. Yamey, eds., *Studies in the History of Accounting*. Homewood, Ill., 1956, pp. 272–87.

Boissonade, M. P. "La Marine marchande, le port et les armateurs de la Rochelle à l'époque de Colbert, 1662–1683," *Bulletin de la section de géographie: Comité des travaux historiques et scientifiques*, XXXVII (1922), 1–45.

Bruchey, Stuart W. "Success and Failure Factors: American Merchants in Foreign Trade in the Eighteenth and Early Nineteenth Centuries," *Business History Review*, XXXII (Autumn 1958), 272–92.

David, Ralph. "Earnings of Capital in the English Shipping Industry, 1670–1730," *Journal of Economic History*, XVII (1957), 409–25.

——. "Merchant Shipping in the Economy of the Late Seventeenth Century," *Economic History Review*, 2d ser., IX (1956), 59–73.

De Foletier, F. De Vaux. "La Rochelle au XVIIIe siècle," *La Nouvelle Revue*, 4th ser., LXIX (Jan.–Feb. 1924), 161–72.

Demos, John. "Families in Colonial Bristol, Rhode Island: An Exercise in Historical Demography," *William and Mary Quarterly,* 3d ser., XXV (Jan. 1968), 40–57.

——. "Underlying Themes in the Witchcraft of Seventeenth Century New England," *American Historical Review,* LXXX (June 1970), 1311–26.

Edsall, T. H. "Something about Fish, Fisheries, and Fishermen in New York in the Seventeenth Century," *New York Genealogical and Biographical Record,* XIII (Oct. 1882), 181–200.

Eno, Joel N. "New York Knickerbocker Families: Origin and Settlement," *New York Genealogical and Biographical Record,* LXV (Oct. 1914), 387–91.

Greven, Philip J., Jr. "Family Structure in Seventeenth-Century Andover, Massachusetts," *William and Mary Quarterly,* 3d ser., XXIII (Apr. 1966), 234–56.

Henretta, James A. "Economic Development and Social Structure in Colonial Boston," *William and Mary Quarterly,* 3d ser., XXII (Jan. 1965), 75–92.

Hoffman, William J. " 'A Tumult of Merchants' of New York in 1698," *New York Genealogical and Biographical Record,* LXXIV (July 1943), 96–100.

Jensen, Richard. "The Religious and Occupational Roots of Party Identification: Illinois and Indiana in the 1870s," *Civil War History,* XVI (Dec. 1970), 325–43.

Johnson, Herbert A. "The Advent of Common Law in Colonial New York," in George A. Billias, ed., *Selected Essays: Law and Authority in Colonial America.* Barre, Mass., 1965, pp. 74–95.

Kammen, Michael G. "The Causes of the Maryland Revolution of 1689," *Maryland Historical Magazine,* LV (Dec. 1960), 293–324.

Kenney, Alice P. "Dutch Patricians in Colonial Albany," *New York History,* XLIX (July 1968), 249–83.

Kerr, John Clapperton. "Some Old Rope Makers and Rope-Walks of New York City," *New York Genealogical and Biographical Record,* LVII (July 1926), 233–36.

Kingdon, Robert M. "Pourquoi les réfugiés huguenots aux colonies américaines, sont-ils devenus épiscopaliens?" *Bulletin de la Société de l'Histoire du Protestantisme Français,* XLII (Oct.–Nov.–Dec. 1969), 487–509.

Klein, Milton M. "Democracy and Politics in Colonial New York," *New York History,* XL (July 1959), 221–46.

Kohler, Max J. "The Civil Status of the Jews in Colonial New York," *American Jewish Historical Society Publications,* no. 6 (1897), 81–106.

Kulikoff, Allan. "The Progress of Inequality in Revolutionary Boston," *William and Mary Quarterly,* 3d ser., XXVIII (July 1971), 375–412.

Kupp, Jan. "Aspects of New York–Dutch Trade under the English,

1670–1674,'' *New-York Historical Society Quarterly,* LVIII (Apr. 1974), 139–47.

Land, Aubrey C. ''Economic Base and Social Structure: The Northern Chesapeake in the Eighteenth Century,'' *Journal of Economic History,* XXV (Dec. 1965), 639–54.

Lazarsfield, Paul F., and Allen H. Barton. ''Qualitative Measurement in the Social Sciences: Classifications, Typologies, and Indices,'' in Daniel Lerner and Harold Lasswell, eds., *The Policy Sciences: Recent Developments in Scope and Method.* Stanford, 1951, pp. 155–92.

Leder, Lawrence H. '' '. . . Like Madmen through the Streets': The New York City Riot of June, 1690,'' *New-York Historical Society Quarterly,* XXXIX (Oct. 1955), 405–15.

——. ''The Politics of Upheaval in New York, 1689–1709,'' *New-York Historical Society Quarterly,* XLIV (Oct. 1960), 413–27.

Le Fevre, Ralph. ''The Huguenots: First Settlers in the Province of New York,'' *Quarterly Journal of the New York Historical Association,* II (1921), 413–27.

Lemisch, Jesse. ''The American Revolution Seen from the Bottom Up,'' in Barton Bernstein, ed., *Towards a New Past.* New York, 1968, pp. 3–45.

——. ''Jack Tar in the Streets: Merchant Seamen in the Politics of Revolutionary America,'' *William and Mary Quarterly,* 3d ser., XXV (July 1968), 371–407.

Lemon, James T., and Gary B. Nash, ''The Distribution of Wealth in Eighteenth-Century America: A Century of Change in Chester County, Pennsylvania, 1693–1802,'' *Journal of Social History,* II (Jan. 1968), 1–24.

Lockridge, Kenneth. ''Land, Population and the Evolution of New England Society, 1630–1790,'' *Past and Present,* no. 39 (Apr. 1968), pp. 62–80.

Lokken, Roy N. ''The Concept of Democracy in Colonial Political Thought,'' *William and Mary Quarterly,* 3d ser., XVI (Oct. 1959), 568–80.

McAnear, Beverly. ''The Place of the Freeman in Old New York,'' *New York History,* XXI (Oct. 1940), 418–30.

McCormick, Richard P. ''Suffrage Classes and Party Alignments: A Study in Voter Behavior,'' *Mississippi Valley Historical Review.* XLVI (Dec. 1959), 397–410.

McCusker, John J. ''Colonial Tonnage Measurement: Five Philadelphia Merchant Ships as a Sample,'' *Journal of Economic History,* XXVIII (Mar. 1967), 82–91.

McGuire, Carson. ''Social Stratification and Mobility Patterns,'' *American Sociological Review,* XV (Apr. 1950), 195–204.

Mason, Bernard. ''Aspects of the New York Revolt of 1689,'' *New York History,* XXX (Apr. 1949), 165–80.

Moore, Charles B. "Shipwrights, Fishermen, Passengers from England," *New York Genealogical and Biographical Record*, X (Apr. 1879), 66–76, (Oct. 1879), 149–55.

Murrin, John. "Review Essay," *History and Theory*, XI (1972), 226–75.

Nash, Gary B. "Slaves and Slaveowners in Colonial Philadelphia," *William and Mary Quarterly*, 3d ser., XXX (Apr. 1973), 223–56.

——. "The Transformation of Urban Politics, 1700–1765," *Journal of American History*, LX (Dec. 1973), 605–32.

Oppenheim, Samuel. "Early History of the Jews in New York, 1654–1664," *American Jewish Historical Society Publications*, no. 18 (1909), pp. 1–91.

Phillips, Rosalie S. "A Burial Place for the Jewish Nation Forever," *American Jewish Historical Society Publications*, no. 18 (1909), pp. 93–132.

Rainbolt, John C. "A 'great and usefull designe': Bellomont's Proposal for New York, 1698–1701," *New-York Historical Society Quarterly*, LIII (Oct. 1969), 333–51.

Runcie, John D. "The Problem of Anglo-American Politics in Bellomont's New York," *William and Mary Quarterly*, 3d ser., XXVI (Apr. 1969), 191–217.

Scott, Kenneth. "The Slave Insurrection in New York in 1712," *New-York Historical Society Quarterly*, XLV (Jan. 1961), 43–74.

Stern, Steve J. "Knickerbockers Who Asserted and Insisted: The Dutch Interest in New York Politics, 1664–1691," *New-York Historical Society Quarterly*, LVIII (Apr. 1974), 113–38.

Swierenga, Robert M. "Ethnocultural Political Analysis: A New Approach to American Ethnic Studies," *Journal of American Studies*, V (Apr. 1971), 59–79.

Syrett, Harold C. "Private Enterprise in New Amsterdam," *William and Mary Quarterly*, 3d ser., XI (Oct. 1954), 536–50.

Tawney, J. J., and R. H. Tawney. "An Occupational Census of the Seventeenth Century," *Economic History Review*, 1st ser., V (Oct. 1934), 25–64.

Totten, John Reynolds. "Consanguinity," *New York Genealogical and Biographical Record*, LXIII (Apr. 1932), 131–44.

Vermilye, A. G. "The Mingling of the Huguenots and Dutch in Early New York," *Proceedings of the Huguenot Society of America*, I (May 1883–June 1884), 24–31.

Villard, Oswald Garrison. "The Early History of Wall Street, 1653–1789," in Maud Wilder Goodwin *et al.*, eds., *Half-Moon Series: Papers on Historic New York*. 2 vols. New York, 1898, I, 102–15.

Wallace, Michael. "Changing Concepts of Party in the United States: New York, 1815–1828," *American Historical Review*, LXXXIV (Dec. 1968), 453–91.

Walton, Gary M. "Colonial Tonnage Measurements: A Comment," *Journal of Economic History,* XXVII (Sept. 1967), 392–97.

———. "Sources of Productivity Change in American Colonial Shipping, 1675–1775," *Economic History Review,* 2d ser., XX (Apr. 1967), 67–78.

Weir, Robert M. " 'The Harmony We Were Famous For': An Interpretation of Pre-Revolutionary South Carolina Politics," *William and Mary Quarterly,* 3d ser., XXVI (Oct. 1969), 473–501.

Wines, Roger A. "William Smith, the Historian of New York," *New York History,* XL (Jan. 1959), 3–17.

Zemsky, Robert M. "Power, Influence, and Status: Leadership Patterns in the Massachusetts Assembly, 1740–1755," *William and Mary Quarterly,* XXVI (Oct. 1969), 502–20.

Zuckerman, Michael. "The Social Context of Democracy in Massachusetts," *William and Mary Quarterly,* 3d ser., XXV (Oct. 1968), 523–44.

Unpublished

Leder, Lawrence H. "Jacob Leisler and the New York Rebellion of 1689–1691." Master's thesis, New York University, 1950.

McAnear, Beverly. "Politics in Provincial New York." Doctoral dissertation, Stanford University, 1932.

Murrin, John. "English Rights as Ethnic Aggression: The English Conquest, The Charter of Liberties of 1683, and Leisler's Rebellion in New York." Mimeographed. Paper presented at American Historical Association Convention, San Francisco, 1973.

☞ *Index*

New York City, 1664–1710

Designed by R. E. Rosenbaum.
Composed by Vail-Ballou Press, Inc.,
in 11 point Linofilm VIP Times Roman, 3 points leaded,
with display lines in Phototypositor Caslon 471.
Printed offset by Vail-Ballou Press
on Warren's No. 66 text, 50 pound basis.
Bound by Vail-Ballou Press
in Joanna book cloth
and stamped in All Purpose foil.